MW01104487

Edition

Escaping the Middle Class
(Canadian Edition)

Secrets to Escaping the Hidden
Job–Mortgage–Tax Trap

Douglas S. Anderson

Order this book online at www.trafford.com/07-1646
or email orders@trafford.com

Most Trafford titles are also available at major online book retailers.

Note for Librarians: A cataloguing record for this book is available from Library and Archives Canada at www.collectionscanada.ca/amicus/index-e.html

Printed in Victoria, BC, Canada.

ISBN: 978-1-4251-4039-7

We at Trafford believe that it is the responsibility of us all, as both individuals and corporations, to make choices that are environmentally and socially sound. You, in turn, are supporting this responsible conduct each time you purchase a Trafford book, or make use of our publishing services. To find out how you are helping, please visit www.trafford.com/responsiblepublishing.html

Our mission is to efficiently provide the world's finest, most comprehensive book publishing service, enabling every author to experience success. To find out how to publish your book, your way, and have it available worldwide, visit us online at www.trafford.com/10510

 www.trafford.com

North America & international
toll-free: 1 888 232 4444 (USA & Canada)
phone: 250 383 6864 ♦ fax: 250 383 6804 ♦ email: info@trafford.com

The United Kingdom & Europe
phone: +44 (0)1865 722 113 ♦ local rate: 0845 230 9601
facsimile: +44 (0)1865 722 868 ♦ email: info.uk@trafford.com

10 9 8 7 6 5 4 3 2

ACKNOWLEDGEMENTS

I'd like to thank my amazing wife Sabrina for all her love and support throughout life and this latest project. Thank you to all my friends and business partners who have inspired me and helped me finish this book. Thanks to Charles Brunet my protégé, while teaching him I learned far more than I could ever have imagined. Thank you Rob Waller, Janice Deroche, Denise Andison, Justin Kohlman, and everyone else who helped polish the final drafts. Thanks goes out to all the good folks at M&M Financial, including Steve McClure, Ross MacFarlane, and Chad Pretsell who have provided me with many initial tools and support necessary to create this book. Thanks goes out to the pioneers in the fields, including John Singleton, Fraser Smith, Sandy Botkin, G. Edward Griffin, T. Harv Eker, Robert Kiyosaki, Donald Trump, and many other great minds and strong spirits. Without your presence on this earth and in my world, a book like this simply would not exist.

Table of Contents

PREFACE

> *Those who say it cannot be done should get out of the way of those who are already doing it.*

— Chinese proverb

I probably don't have to tell you that days spent in the middle class are like a hamster running incessantly on a wheel. Millions of Canadians spend every day going through the same scenario never getting ahead. And like the hamster on a wheel, they are completely ignorant of the fact that they are even going in circles. They will only know the implications of their wheel when they try to retire and watch their quality of life slowly spin to a halt. You on the other hand are about to be freed from the middle class trap. Knowledge is power and once you realize you are trapped, this book will help you plan an exit strategy. Interestingly, you will realize that the same traps that have been keeping you in the middle class can help catapult you into a bigger and better life than you may have ever imagined. Akin to how the aikido warrior who uses the enemy's energy to his own advantage, the middle class escape artist uses the mediocrity of the middle class to escape his own traps with ease.

This book challenges the accepted social financial norms. It bucks the trend. It encourages strategies to maximize cash flow and minimize taxes. Some of the concepts described to help make this happen go against the grain, such as owing money on your house, getting a 100 percent tax refund, avoiding mutual funds, making guaranteed double digit returns or higher on all your investments, and being free to leave a job well before retirement age. If that sounds counter intuitive or even impossible, this book is meant especially for you. Once these preconceived notions of *impossible* are turned into *possible*, then all of the actions described in this book can be geared towards raising capital to generate income in order to become financially free – in less than a decade.

The reason there is a need for this book is simple: they don't teach this stuff in school, or at the various learning institutions for finance. You won't get this information by taking a MBA, or studying to become a financial advisor. Those teachings already exist in the box, and you have to leave the box in order to make progress. What we often don't understand is that the exit directions are written on the outside of the box, where we can't see them. This book will take you outside of the box so you can read the instructions, and enjoy the benefits for yourself.

The longer people keep swallowing the same "traditional" strategies, the harder it will get to escape the middle class – and the gap between the haves and have nots in Canada will continue to widen. If you don't position yourself to advance your wealth, you will find yourself at the lower end of the wealth gap and be amongst the vast majority of people who retire in poverty.

So how do you get out of the box and escape the middle class traps? First, you've got to discover you are trapped. Then, work with others who think differently about wealth creation – people like the main character in this book – people who have actually retired early and wealthy. Would you rather settle for an *advisor* who simply talks and plans for financial freedom or learn from a *mentor* who has already travelled to where you want to be? The best credential is not a piece of paper on the wall – it is the status of financial freedom. Find as many mentors as you can who understand your desires and goals, then do what they did, and your progress will be rapid.

This book is a no-nonsense guide for the large majority of society with moderate means (i.e. the "middle class") to escape the accepted norm and accelerate their financial liberty. Why write a book specifically for the middle class? First, wealthy individuals have usually solved the problems presented in this book (although I have met some who still find elements of this information to be new). Second, this book requires a mortgage, substantial taxes, and considerable bills to be used as tools for financial freedom – something the lower income earners typically don't have. Those in the middle class pay most of the taxes, hold most of the mortgages, and are the closest (yet the farthest) to becoming truly wealthy.

From personal experience, I can tell you financial freedom should take no more than a decade, and certainly not the conventional 30 or 40 years that other books or traditional media will tell you it will take. This timetable is accelerated, but it is not to be confused with get-rich-quick. It is however, also better than getting poor slowly like most conventional thinking steers people towards. In just the first few years of my personal escape from the middle class traps, I managed to save tens of thousands of dollars in income tax and turn that into hundreds of thousands of dollars worth of investments. If I can do that in a few years before the age of 30, I believe anybody else can also do it at any age in under a decade.

What I've learned came in bits and pieces from observing, thinking, learning, and doing. Only after going through this process myself was I able to see all the pieces of the puzzle and rearrange the order and assemble them in the most optimal way. This book therefore combines the benefit of my hindsight and the knowledge of those from whom I've learned.

I chronicle these strategies through the eyes of a composite character named Mike. You can observe the thoughts and decisions he has made, and decide for yourself what applies to you, and what you will implement in your life. Whatever works for your situation, by all means use it right away. It is also helpful to discuss the topics with others, so I recommend sharing them with a few people who are also interested in financial freedom. I have found discussing these strategies, ideas, and tools with others to be most helpful in understanding them.

In closing, I would like to invite you on this journey into financial freedom. I have become a huge fan of learning from others as much as possible, leveraging their knowledge and experience, shortcutting the course of learning, and trying not to repeat their mistakes. I hope you can use this book in the same way. I have seen many people blaze new and radical paths, and I hope this book motivates you to grow and learn from these ideas and perhaps blaze new paths of your own. I encourage you to share your successes with us so that we may post them to www.yourleverage.com.

WHO IS THIS MIKE GUY?

> *"Human beings, who are almost unique in having the ability to learn from the experience of others, are also remarkable for their apparent disinclination to do so."*
>
> – Douglas Adams
> English author (1952 - 2001)

Meet Millionaire Mike. He's an engineer, and self-taught financial number cruncher. He also became financially free in less than one decade using the tools described in this book. He was not a dot-com super kid or a genius entrepreneur. He just knew how to turn hidden traps into financial gems. This is his story.

1

Mike wasn't always financially free. In fact, a short time ago Mike didn't think he could ever have so much wealth coming into his life with so little effort. This is Mike's journey of escaping from the middle class traps. Pay close attention, because if you have a mortgage, income tax, and personal bills to pay like Middle Class Mike did, you could also escape in several short years without reducing your standard of living along the way.

Mike had a pretty normal upbringing. He finished high school with good grades in a town outside of Vancouver near the Washington-British Columbia border. Finishing school and getting a good job had always been his goal since he was a child, as his parents had planted that seed in his mind. And he did what had to be done to meet his goal. He studied engineering in university. He got a good, secure, stable job at an established engineering firm and was promoted to a middle management position where he often commuted back and forth between their Vancouver and Seattle offices.

Having now met his lifelong goal he realized it wasn't what he had been expecting. Work was going well and it paid the bills, but he hit a mental wall. Now, as he got up too early, to work too hard, for too long, for too little gratitude, he began wondering if this is all life was about. He realized that his employment was going to keep him busy, but it wasn't going to give him options to live life on his own terms. He wasn't at a mid-life crisis looking to buy a red sports car, but he was left feeling that life was passing him by and so were innumerable opportunities. He decided to embark on a new goal – to be wealthy enough to spend his time doing what he wanted, not what others demanded of him.

"But where do I start?" Mike asked himself over and over again. Mike wasn't wealthy, and he learned that only a small percentage of the population was truly rich. It seemed the first step quite simply had to be to figure out money. Mike had always been told you couldn't control something if you don't understand it. It seemed logical that money was the same. If he was to have enough money to be financially free he had to understand how it worked, so he wouldn't have to.

Figuring out money was no small feat. Even understanding what others thought about money was a bit overwhelming. A trip to the bookstore was like going to a large grocery store. There was obviously everything you could possibly need to satisfy your financial appetite, but also way more than one person could hope to devour. Nonetheless, he did his best and read those books that were rated online as the most successful. It was tremendously overwhelming, but it was a good start.

> "*Knowledge will forever govern ignorance; and a people who mean to be their own governors must arm themselves with the power which knowledge gives.*"
>
> - James Madison
> Fourth President of the United States (1809-1817)

One of the messages that repeatedly came up in his reading was that if you are to be rich, you must think like a rich person. The people who Middle Class Mike hung out with were not much help in this regard. He knew a wide selection of people who almost seemed afraid to talk about money at all. His parents, who told him to work hard, save lots and get a good job, had sent him on his career path to engineering but were of little help when it came to learning about money. Rick, his financial advisor and mutual fund salesman, had less money than he did. His friends ranged from people who thought Mike was greedy for wanting to become a millionaire, to those who encouraged him fully – they encouraged him to loan them money once he was wealthy. Indeed, the people Middle Class Mike spent time with were good friends, but he quickly discovered that if he was to move ahead he had to spend time with those who could teach him what he needed to know. This isn't to say he had to end his current friendships, but he did have to branch out. In the working world, it's considered normal to "network" or make friends with those who can teach you the ropes and help you succeed. Mike discovered the same could be true in the personal finance world.

As he made friends with those who were interested in building wealth, they explained to him the golden rule of understanding money: in order to make money you need time and knowledge. But they didn't tell him to buy investments, hold them for 40 years and hope that they go up in value so he could retire. Quite the opposite. They counselled him to break his original goal of "figuring out money" into two more specific objectives. First, he was tutored to become financially free. In other words, find ways to generate income that didn't require him to work for it (known as passive income) that would replace the income from his day job so he could concentrate his time on finding and making good financial decisions. As a well-paid engineer, this actually takes longer than it would for someone who makes less, but as his new friends had personally demonstrated, it still should never take more than ten years. Then, once that big hurdle was overcome, Mike could focus on using his new-found time to make good investments that would allow Mike to enjoy life at a much higher level then any middle-class Canadian could hope for.

For the first time since he left university, the 28-year-old engineer felt the spark of excitement flow in his blood that only an ambitious goal can provide. He had a first goal: to be in a financial position that would allow him to become financially free in less than 10 years. He still had a mortgage, bills to pay, and a job that paid as much in tax as he was paying for his mortgage, but he had a new goal in life. Now, he just had to find a way to generate a passive income that matched his current salary.

He nicknamed his journey "escaping the middle class", and it started with figuring out what traps were holding the middle class back from financial freedom.

IDENTIFYING THE TRAPS

"My brain is the key that sets my mind free."

- Harry Houdini
Magician, Escapologist, and Stunt Performer (1874 – 1926)

SPRINGING THE TRAPS

As he was thinking about his first goal, Mike watched a fly trying to leave the kitchen through the window. The window was open on one side, but the fly was buzzing blindly against the glass pane on the other side. Even though the fly could see outside, it couldn't get there. The fly had no idea that a just few inches away was its freedom. Mike brushed his hand at the fly trying to usher it outside, but the fly quickly flew around his hand staying pressed against the impenetrable glass. In that moment Mike realized that one of his first tasks toward his goal of becoming financially free was to simply figure out where the traps are located. Unlike the fly, he had no intention of continually ramming himself into a wall until he discovered a way out. He would step back, take a look at how he was trapped and then figure out a strategic exit plan.

Coming to that conclusion didn't take long. Finding the traps on the other hand did take a while. Over the following months Mike continued to read and to talk to his new mentoring wealthy friends. And he developed a habit of asking questions. His entire life he had been told things that were assumed to be truth. But as he questioned these "truths" he started to get a better understanding of where the traps were lying hidden.

SPOT THE HIDDEN MIDDLE CLASS TRAPS

Mike also began to realize that traps existed within the traps. In other words there were often layers of false assumptions protecting bad middle class habits. Though he found it discouraging to think he had found his way out of one only to find another trap, he also found the more he did this, the easier it became. He also learned to stop buzzing around long enough to see some openings materialize. Instead of just being busy, he was focusing on being productive. If the middle class gap was going to continue widening[1], then he was intent on ensuring he was among the few that got richer, not among the masses who were getting poorer.

Mike could see how easy it was to take the path of least resistance to join the soon-to-be-poor middle class. Mike's co-worker Samantha and her husband Harry couldn't be bothered looking into building their wealth. They spent most of what they earned and blindly invested small amounts at tax time in traditional avenues hoping for good results. Sam and Harry made good money and had their house nearly paid off. Harry was a successful entrepreneur and Sam was an engineer Mike worked with. Yet they were living month-to-month and would be in deep financial trouble if they missed a month's pay. Unless they were willing to live with less in the future, their hope of retiring by the age of 60 was almost nonexistent. Mike imagined how much worse it was for his friends who lived on debt, racking up credit cards or living beyond their means. They had no future and their present was a short-lived financial illusion.

Why are middle class families such as Samantha and Harry stuck? What is keeping them from becoming financially free or wealthy? To Mike this was the key question. What are the traps keeping people like Sam and Harry stuck on a financial hamster wheel just

[1] Statistics Canada, *Perspective on Labour and Income*, February 2002, Vol.3, No.2 and GROWING GAP, GROWING CONCERNS, Canadian Attitudes Toward Income Inequality, November 20, 2006

earning enough to survive, but never enough to thrive? It always seemed easier to see these problems in others' lives. But before he could help others, he had to help himself.

Combining the problem solving skills he developed as an engineer, with the finance skills he had built by studying finances on a part-time basis, Mike started to try and uncover the traps in the most methodical way possible.

This meant starting at the beginning with the basics. Mike sat down and took a hard look at what assets and liabilities he had, and how his monthly income was being spent. This is what his basic personal balance sheet looked like:

Middle Class Mike's Balance Sheet

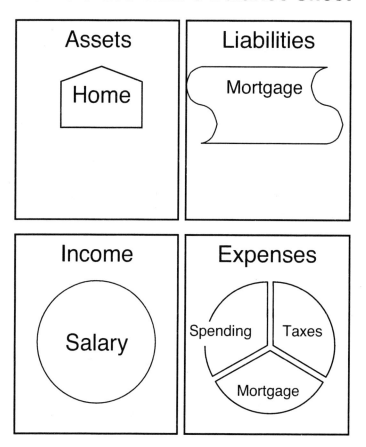

The only thing Mike had of any value was his personal home, which was offset by the mortgage he owed the bank. His only source of income was the salary from his job, and he spent most of his after-tax salary on what he thought were necessary expenses.

Let's take a closer look at how his money was being spent:

Middle Class Mike's Expenses

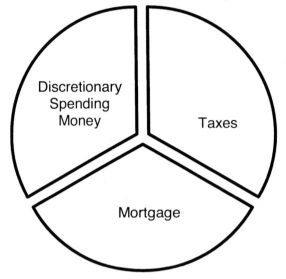

A third of his income was taken from him in the form of income taxes before he even saw it, a third disappeared into his mortgage payment, and the rest of the discretionary money was spent on bills.

Most critical of all, if he stopped working, his house and spending money would be gone because his income came from a single source – his salary. In Mike's engineering world, his single income would be called a "single point of failure" – meaning that if he lost that one item, he'd lose 100 percent of his income. Not only did he have very little cash for himself at the end of the month, his entire lifestyle was susceptible to collapse if he lost his job or became unable to work. This is consistent with other middle class families he knew, who are on average just a few paycheques away from bankruptcy due to their high debt and low savings.[2]

It didn't take a rocket scientist – make that rocket *engineer* – for Mike to realize his current situation wasn't that different than that of Sam and Harry. Many of the same things he took pride in - his home, his country and his job - were holding him back from moving forward. But he would find a way – his financial life literally depended on it.

> By 2005, for each dollar of disposable income, Canadians owed $1.16 and Americans $1.24.
>
> Source: Bank of Canada, and US Federal Reserve

FALLING FOR THE MORTGAGE TRAP

Springing the traps is all about spotting the traps, and the first sieve in Mike's bank account was his mortgage. Since an enormous amount of capital was leaving his pocket every month, the question was, "how could this negative situation be turned into a positive one?" Restructuring his mortgage to make it tax efficient and more importantly, to let him access capital was easier than he expected. Mike figured that he might as well make his mortgage work *for* him, instead of *against* him. With a little research Mike figured out that his mortgage could be restructured to create cash flow and extended tax benefits. In Chapter 3 we will see exactly *why* it was better for Mike to restructure his

[2] Data from the U.S. Federal Reserve, 2004 and Statistics Canada, 2007

mortgage rather than leave it in the usual traditional form. In Chapter 4 we will see exactly *how* Mike converted his home into a massive source of capital which at the same time boosted his tax refunds.

AFRAID OF THE TAX TRAP?

The second major drain on Mike's pocketbook was the Income Tax Act. Mike discovered that the Canada Revenue Agency uses fear, ignorance, coercion, and extortion to get its job done. But more importantly, he also learned from books like *Tackling the Taxman* by Alex Doulis or the *Ten Secrets Revenue Canada Doesn't Want You to Know* by David M. Voth that taxes aren't as inevitable as most people believe. Mike discovered that he could use both his own bills and even other people's bills to substantially reduce his own taxes. Mike set out to do just that – reduce the amount of income tax he owed.

> "When the people fear their government, there is tyranny; when the government fears the people, there is liberty."
>
> - Thomas Jefferson
> Third President of the United States

What made Mike recognize that taxes are a middle class trap was the understanding that there were easy and legal ways to reduce the amount of tax payable. Chapter 5 explores how Mike used his *own* bills to save taxes. Chapter 6 is even more fun – it looks at how Mike quickly and easily got help from *others* to save an enormous amount of tax.

INVESTING AGAINST THE CROWD

The third trap was perhaps the most critical to spot. Mortgage payments and taxes have been lamented for centuries – spotting them was not a problem. However, the final major trap was traditional investment vehicles.

For decades, Canadians have been trained to just ignorantly hand their money over to the stock market and hope it grows. But the fact is, most of the so-called "tried and true" methods of investing, are only tried and trued for those selling the investment vehicles. However, because most middle-class Canucks place their faith in these vehicles to deliver their golden retirement to them on a platter, they are reluctant to question it.

"This is what everyone else does, it must be the right answer," is the typical way of thinking. But in fact Mike found that swimming upstream while everyone else is swimming downstream didn't mean he was swimming toward his demise. On the contrary, it meant he was floating to financial freedom while the majority of people had a lot of hard paddling in front of them later in life just to stay afloat.

Chapter 7 uncovers how Mike changed his investment mentality to open up a wider range of investment options. Chapter 8 shows how he weighed the options and chose those that would deliver the best results for him.

Once Mike had sprung these traps, he was well on his way to becoming Millionaire Mike. But we are getting ahead of ourselves. First, Mike had to spring his mortgage trap.

THE MORTGAGE MYTH

> *"Worm or beetle - drought or tempest - on a farmer's land may fall. Each is loaded full of ruin, but a mortgage beats them all."*
>
> - Will Carleton
> American poet (1845 - 1912)

BIGGEST MISTAKE OF YOUR FINANCIAL LIFE

"But we're already Millionaires," Samantha explained to Mike, raising up her hands in a model-like-pose to show off her newly remodelled kitchen, complete with the new cappuccino maker. "We have half this mortgage paid off, and this house is appraised at more than a million dollars."

"Exactly," her husband Harry added with pride. "In a dozen more years, we'll have the whole mortgage paid off and we'll have the best investment of our lives right over our heads."

Mike had intentionally come to talk to Samantha and Harry because he knew they strongly believed that their home was their biggest financial asset. He knew that if he could talk to them in detail he could understand all the arguments and then analyze the situation. Mike intended to test the theories and see if they held up to scrutiny. And this kitchen was the best place to start. He wanted to understand if buying a private home was really the economic sanctuary so many middle class Canadians claimed.

> *One of the biggest myths in the middle class today is that a fully paid home is the best investment you can make.*

"You see, house prices increase over time," Harry continued. "The rise in the value of an asset is called *appreciation* in investment terms. This rise in the price of our house – in other words, the appreciation – is where our investment makes us money. Home appreciation is just like a rising stock market, where you can buy low, and then sell high later. The difference being, we can live in this house while it is increasing in price."

Recent skyrocketing prices in the real estate market only made the two more convinced of the wisdom of their logic. And many others seemed to concur. Most of Mike's other middle class friends also thought that they should pay off their mortgage before even thinking about investing. But yet, Mike couldn't help but think of the fact that in spite of this so-called wealth, Samantha and Harry had confided in him several times that they could hardly make ends meet. Every month was a struggle just to pay the bills. By paying off their home, they were investing in their home. But if their million-dollar home was sucking them dry, was it truly a good investment?

Mike started his research by looking at historic home prices, because at first the best indication of whether a home is a good investment seemed to be looking to history. Most people would figure if the price went up over the past it's a good deal. If prices went down it's a bad deal. To determine if this argument was in fact valid, Mike decided to get a historical perspective by looking at an individual situation: that of his uncle.

Mike's Uncle Stuart bought a house in 1950 for $35,000 that was selling for $350,000 in 2005. Uncle Stuart thought that it was a great investment – the best

Inflation is the rising cost of living over time.

he had ever made. After all, he had 10 times more value in his house compared to what he paid for it. However, if it also cost Stuart 10 times more for a loaf of bread, was he really any farther ahead? Was the house a great investment, or just a really large piggy bank? Did his money really grow in *purchasing power*, or was it just sitting there growing at the same rate as his cost to live? The fact is, in Uncle Stuart's case, he gained no real growth at all, as he couldn't buy any more items in 2005 than he could in 1950. All of his gains were wiped out by the rising cost of living, known as inflation. Think about all the real lost opportunity for growth in his purchasing power.

Researchers from the Massachusetts Institute of Technology (MIT) named Wheaton and Baranski have proven that over time homes show no gain in price beyond inflation.[3] This doesn't mean that home prices never rise faster than the rate of inflation, it simply means over the long term they don't. There are occasional sustained up swings and down swings in real prices in certain regions over particular periods in time, but in the long run the real value never changes.

---

[3] *100 years of Commercial Real Estate prices in Manhattan*, May, 1 2006, Wheaton, Baranski, MIT

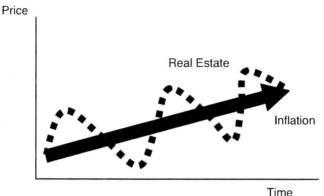

For example, after adjusting for inflation, Wheaton and Baranski showed that Manhattan commercial office property values were 30 percent lower in 1999 than they were in 1899. If in this situation the real estate was used as a pure appreciation investment, relying only on the price increasing in order to buy low and sell high, the seller would only be able to buy 70 percent of the amount of goods and services that could have been purchased 100 years earlier. The same lack of growth past inflation has been seen in residential real estate – or in this case, in Mike's home.

In particular, Mike discovered that having a home paid for is an especially poor investment. He found if the home is paid off all the money that has been paid for the home is simply sitting in the house as equity and is not growing at all. If the house is paid off, it is a terrible waste of capital, and an

> **Equity** is the money that is stored in the house.

even worse investment strategy. After all, any equity in his house was doomed to grow only at the rate of inflation over the long term.

After becoming enlightened about these home investment facts, Mike wanted to figure out if it's possible to determine when real estate is approaching a high or low point in its long term cycle. The recent rapid rise in the housing market in North America seemed to have no bounds, but he wanted to know if that was indeed true or if there was data that could inform what might happen to prices in the future.

He decided to wade through the history books to determine what has happened to housing in the past and how that might inform Mike about the future.

WHO ERASED MORTGAGES FROM THE HISTORY BOOKS?

Mike started digging into history to find out what he could about mortgages in the past. The first thing he found is that before 1930, mortgage periods were much shorter – between 5 and 10 years long. Also before 1930, those who owned houses had also put at least a 50 percent down payment on the house.[4]

---

[4] *The American Mortgage in Historical and International Context*, Richard K. Green and Susan M. Wachter, INSTITUTE FOR LAW AND ECONOMICS, University of Pennsylvania Law School, 2005

This meant that before 1930, a family buying a house was able to save half the price of the house, and then pay off the rest of the house within several years. Relative to the average income at that time, this meant that house was really quite affordable. Indeed, real estate got more expensive between 1930 and today – but why? What happened? Even more importantly: is it likely to continue?

The Great Depression changed many aspects of the economy, including affordable housing. During the 1920s, the banks had lowered interest rates to abnormally low levels, triggering massive borrowing and speculation in the stock market. Suddenly, right around 1929, the banking community raised interest rates from historic lows to a significantly higher rate of six percent.[5] The loans were called in and the stock market crashed, but a less publicized crash in the history books was the real estate market crash.

Despite having more than half of the house paid off, many banks would not renew the mortgage on houses because they knew the mortgage amount owed was more than the house was worth in the new real estate market. The banks demanded that the borrower pay off the mortgage in full using cash. Of course, many people couldn't pay off the full amount of the mortgage upon the yearly renewal, and were forced to hand over their homes to the bank. Not surprisingly, during the

---

[5] pg 498, The Creature from Jekyll Island, G. E. Griffin

first part of the 1930's, more than half of the mortgaged homes went into foreclosure.

The government took over the foreclosures from the banks and wanted to get these houses back into homeowners' hands. However, under current terms (six percent interest with a five to ten year loan length) the monthly payments were still unaffordable because wages had also dropped in the 1930's – if you still had a job. What the government did to make housing affordable again was to stretch out the amortization period[6] from a maximum of 10 years to a maximum of 20. This was later extended to 30 years and longer. Although the mortgage *amount* on the house was the same, the longer loan *period* lowered the monthly payment amount, making it affordable once again.

After the Great Depression ended and wages adjusted, the increased affordability eventually balanced out with higher home prices. Since the loan term was much longer, there was considerably more interest to pay, so the price of the house was relatively more expensive compared to wages.

Mike looked at the prices of houses for the past several decades, and it really looked as if the prices rose substantially over that period. But what really happened in the 1930's was the beginning of the restructuring of mortgage terms to make the same house more affordable to someone who was now earning less.

---

[6] Amortization period is the length of the mortgage

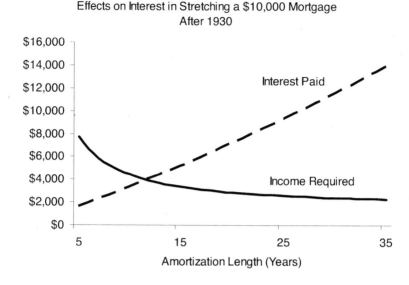

Effects on Interest in Stretching a $10,000 Mortgage
After 1930

The prices had been buoyed up by affordability, as if the bankers and politicians were pulling levers on a huge mortgage machine pumping out money for homes.

These days mortgage features continue to be stretched even further to make them even *more* affordable. Mike kept in mind that "more affordable" meant that the buying side of the market can push the house price up even further, giving it an apparent "rise" in value. However, these artificial factors created by the banks to get even more interest out of the middle class reaches a limit. This means that prices can only be pushed up from lower interest rates, longer amortization, and lower down payments for so long.

The levers can only be pulled on the machine until they max out. That only leaves one main factor to affect the price of homes: wages.

PRICE FACTORS

Mike figured that when house prices rise, there has to be a driving force to fund the demand. In other words, what affects how much money people have available to spend on a home? Mike narrowed it down to three major factors that affect prices.

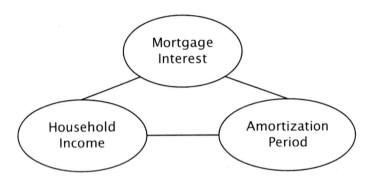

Mortgage lending amounts depend on these basic factors:

- Mortgage interest rates,
- Amortization period, and
- Household income

INTEREST RATES

In 2004, interest rates began hitting multi-decade lows, and Mike began to observe rates approach the lower limit. Interest-only mortgages became available, which allowed even more people to buy a house for a lower monthly payment.

Mike knew that the interest rate directly affects affordability. Mike's former apartment roommate Lucy couldn't qualify for a $250,000 mortgage at 6% interest rates in the past because she needed to earn $50,000 in order to afford it – but she only earned $40,00 per year. But as rates dropped to 5% percent she could afford the same $250,000 mortgage amount on her $40,000 salary. The more the interest rates dropped, the less she was required to earn to qualify for the same mortgage amount. This increased her affordability, fuelled the demand, and raised prices.

Interest rates had been generally declining from 1980 to 2004, gradually increasing affordability and pushing up home prices compared to wages. However, this can only go so far, as once interest rates hit rock bottom, interest rates cease to be a factor in affordability under normal economic circumstances.

Technically 0% interest could eventually be introduced, but that would provide no motivation for the lender to loan the money.

Eventually interest rates reach a point where they cannot be lowered any further and allow the lender to still make a profit. Even more interesting is that the lower interest rates go, the less of an effect the change has on affordability.

Effects of Lowering Interest Rate by 1%

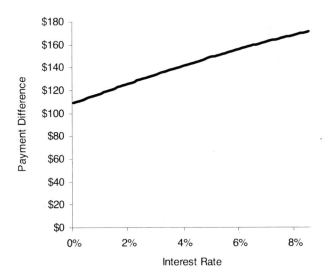

What does this mean? It means that lowering the rate from 8% to 7% makes the mortgage payment $162 lower, but lowering 2% to 1% only makes the payment $117 lower.[7] The lower the interest rate, the less the effect when it changes, even if it is lowered by the same percentage amount.

Since there was very little room between the current rates and 0%, Mike believed this would no longer be a major factor in raising the prices of housing. If anything, interest rates had nowhere to go but up, making housing less affordable and causing house prices to fall.

---

[7] $250,000 Mortgage for 25 Years, although the difference will be proportional to any mortgage amount for any duration.

AMORTIZATION

The amortization period is the length of the mortgage loan. Mike saw that the amortization lever on the mortgage machine had also been pulled to the maximum limit.

As he had learned during his research on the Great Depression, when the length of mortgages went from 5 years to 20 years, it had a *huge* effect on lowering the monthly payments. However, lengthening from 20 to 35 years has less of an effect. Lengthening from 35 to 50 years has even less effect. Going all the way to 100 year mortgage doesn't really lower the monthly payment very much at all, except it does put more money in the bank's pocket in the form of interest payments. Interest only mortgages have an infinite amortization, where interest will always be paid but the mortgage principle will never be paid off.

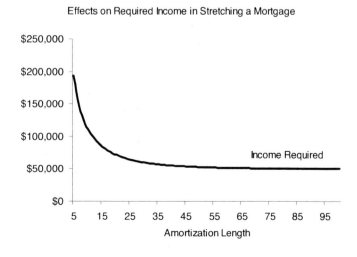

Mike crunched Lucy's numbers using a $250,000 mortgage at 6% interest as an example. How much did she have to earn in order to qualify for this mortgage? How much could her qualifying yearly earnings lower as he increased the amortization period? It turns out Lucy would always have to earn at least $50,000 in order to qualify for this mortgage, even if the mortgage was stretched to 1,000 years!

Once the amortization level on the mortgage machine reached 50 years or more, the affordability levelled out at about $50,000 per year income required to afford the mortgage at 6% interest. This meant that since Lucy earned only $40,000 she could not just ask the bank to add a few more years to the mortgage length so that she could afford it. Here this mortgage factor hits the floor, and there is no more room to move. Mike determined that lengthening the period of the mortgage any further no longer has an effect on price.

WAGES, DUAL INCOMES, AND INVESTMENTS

Back in 1930, there was typically only one income coming into the house. During World War II, women began to enter the workforce, and by the 1970s there was a strong trend towards the dual income family – both husband and wife. With twice as much income, the family could now afford more house – in theory. Unfortunately, since nearly *everyone* could afford more, this caused increased borrowing to buy higher priced houses, so all prices rose due to inflation. Today, a dual income household is almost always required in order to afford the same house that was easily afforded by a single income earner 50 years ago.

Fellow trap springers Elizabeth Warren and Amelia Warren Tyagi explain in their book *The Two-Income Trap: Why Middle-Class Mothers and Fathers Are Going Broke*:

> *"The average two-income family earns far more today than did the single-breadwinner family of a generation ago. And yet, once they have paid the mortgage, the car payments, the taxes, the health insurance, and the day-care bills, today's dual-income families have less discretionary — and less money to put away for a rainy day — than the single-income family of a generation ago."*

So, unless the kids are going to start to work and pitch in with the mortgage costs, income has also become a limiting factor to drive up prices. Although, judging by the results of the dual income family, adding a third income to society would not likely make matters any better.

Essentially, since the price of housing is linked to mortgages, and mortgages are linked to wages and inflation, housing is eternally linked to inflation and wages. Mike was seeing the fundamentals behind why a home wasn't a good investment for capital. When we invest at rates near inflation, we're really not investing at all as the money doesn't grow in purchasing power.

ALL THINGS REMAINING EQUAL

So after all this research, Mike was back where he started. If mortgage rates can't fall and longer terms won't make housing more affordable then the only thing that can increase housing prices is increased household income. Household income tends to rise with inflation. All of this is consistent with what Mike found the researchers Wheaton and Baranski from MIT have proven to happen over the past hundred years in several different countries in their research report.

Aside from just the price of the house increasing over time, let's take a deeper look at *why* Mike figured that investing in a paid off house wasn't a great idea.

APPRECIATION COSTS A FORTUNE

Many of Mike's friends loved the fact that their houses appreciated in value. What they neglected to look at was the cost of that appreciation, which just adds to the mortgage trap. For any venture, including investing in a home, to find out how much is really gained – or lost – all the factors must be added together, including the cost for this "investment."

To determine whether anything is profitable or not, Mike used this formula:

Gross Gain – Costs = Net Gain (or Loss)

Mike found that most people tended to just look at the gross gain of the appreciation of the house, but totally ignore the costs. Samantha and Harry were claiming their home was a million dollar asset. What had it cost them? If it cost them $2 million was it still a good deal? There are significant costs to obtain this home appreciation, and they must be taken into account every time.

Mike already looked at the cost of inflation, which cancels the house appreciation in the long run. Other costs included interest, maintenance, insurance, taxes, and lost opportunity. Ignoring the "smaller" costs of taxes, maintenance and insurance, the big three costs of interest, inflation and opportunity lost alone were staggering.

The interest on a mortgage debt is one major cost. Later on, we'll see how Mike decided to "borrow to invest" something which many people seem to fear. But really, any mortgage holder who sees his house as an investment is already borrowing to invest. Since modern day amortization is decades long, interest is a large cost to purchasing a home and cannot be ignored.

As Mike found out earlier inflation is the lost purchasing power of dollars year over year. Therefore inflation only affects year-to-year savings, so it essentially only affects[8] the portion of the house that is

---

[8] Technically, inflation also applies to the mortgaged portion of the house too. But since both the appreciation and loan are reduced in value by the effects of inflation, they cancel each other out.

paid off (the "equity"). The interest costs, however, only applies to the part of the house that is still mortgaged and not the part of the house that is paid off.

Thus, Mike viewed the house as divided in two parts: the part that is still mortgaged, and the part that is full of equity. As time passes, the mortgage gradually gets paid off and the weight shifts from the left to the right. The following illustration shows this split.

Taking into account the costs involved to own a home, the net gain (or loss) can be calculated using a simple formula:

Gain		% Mortgaged		% Equity
(or)	=	X	+	X
Loss		(Appreciation – Interest)		(Appreciation – Inflation)

Mike looked at the left hand side first – the mortgaged side. The interest rate that lenders charge is usually greater than the published rate of inflation (rate of inflation plus a few percentage points). In Mike's case it was inflation plus 3%. On the right hand side – the equity side – long term gain equals inflation, as proven by history, so the homeowner basically breaks even here. Adjusting the formula, it becomes:

$$\text{Appreciation} = \text{Inflation}$$
$$\text{(and)}$$
$$\text{Interest} = \text{Inflation} + 3\%$$

Gain (or) Loss	=	% Mortgaged X (Inflation – Inflation – 3%)	+	% Equity X (Inflation – Inflation)

The gain or loss becomes:

Gain (or) Loss	=	% Mortgaged X – 3%	+	% Equity X 0

What does this mean? The part of the house that is mortgaged loses 3% every year, and the equity gains are lost to inflation so it doesn't grow at all (0%). Instead it acts like a hungry piggy bank that can't be spent.

But the story doesn't end there. As a mortgage is being paid off, less interest is being paid on the mortgage principle, but more equity is being stored in the house. Each dollar stored in the house is another dollar that *could be* invested wisely, but isn't. The rate of return on this money that wasn't invested is called "Lost Opportunity."

Changing Mortgage Cost Over Time

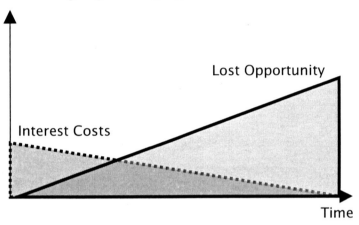

In reality, Mike also needed to subtract the lost opportunity from any equity held in the house. Not only is this money just sitting there barely keeping up with inflation, it isn't being put to good use. Accounting for lost opportunity, the situation becomes:

Gain (or) Loss	=	% Mortgaged X (Appreciation − Interest)	+	% Equity X (Appreciation − Inflation − Lost Opportunity)

Substituting as before, this becomes:

Gain (or) Loss	=	% Mortgaged X − 3%	+	% Equity X − Lost Opportunity

Mike thought of lost opportunity as the garage that he could have had if the equity in the house was put to good use as investment capital. This garage would be holding the Ferrari that he could be driving, in the better part of town that he could be living in, around better schools that the kids could be going to. Even though lost opportunity isn't a tangible loss, it is a real cost of not investing the capital wisely. Lost opportunity can be likened to inflation. Although the money doesn't change in amount, the value disappears quietly over time. The motto for lost opportunity's is "Shoulda, woulda, coulda."

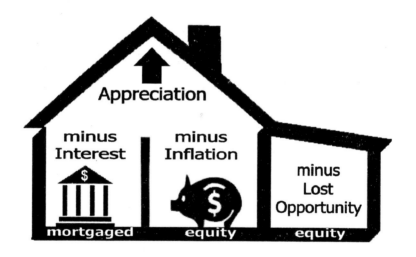

Thus, the overall real return of investing in a home in the long run is generally negative, and the investment return gets more negative as the mortgage is paid off. In reality, a home is a consumer item, as it consumes wealth if not structured properly.

The good news was that if Mike seized the opportunity instead of losing it, his negative house return would change into positive returns and his house wouldn't be such a bad investment.

"But mortgage payments eventually disappear, compared to renters who will always be paying rent," Mike's friend Lenny said to him, using old-world arguments trying to dismiss Mike's findings.

Lenny had no mortgage payments because he had his mortgage paid off. Mike reminded Lenny that this meant that he was investing in his house at the rate of inflation – which meant he wasn't really making any money. Since he was also losing the opportunity to invest this money – *really* invest this money – it was in fact costing him a lot more in lost opportunity than it was saving him in mortgage payments. Lenny's paid off house was worth $250,000. Mike showed Lenny how he could safely get a net return of 11% on his $250,000 from an investment, and that Lenny was losing to opportunity to earn $27,500 per year.

Since Lenny was saving only $13,096 per year in mortgage payments, having a paid off house actually cost

> **Where could the net 11% come from?**
>
> *Lenny could have easily purchased a nearby $1 million apartment building that was for sale with his $250,000 as a down payment. The $42,500 in rent would have given him 17% return, less the 6% in interest is was costing his to borrow the money – giving him 11% net return of $27,500.*

him $14,404 in just the first year.[9]

Running all of Lenny's numbers, Mike showed him how he could have no worries for retirement if Lenny wisely used the equity in his house. Mike even made the comparison assuming that Lenny would invest the mortgage payments he was saving by having his mortgage paid off.

Lenny's Paid-Off Home "Lost Opportunity"

	Paid Off & Appreciating House Equity	Appreciation Gain Only	Appreciation + Invested Mortgage Payments	Appreciation + Invested Home Equity
Start	$250,000	$0	$0	0
Year 1	$275,000	$25,000	$38,096	$52,500
Year 2	$302,500	$52,500	$80,132	$141,025
Year 3	$332,750	$82,750	$126,517	$272,563
Year 4	$366,025	$116,025	$177,702	$455,172
Year 5	$402,628	$152,628	$234,185	$698,131
Year 6	$442,890	$192,890	$296,515	$1,012,105
Year 7	$487,179	$237,179	$365,299	**$1,409,334**

In Lenny's first option, he gets a generous 10% appreciation on the value of his house every year, starting at $25,000. The second option is the same, except Mike assumed Lenny also invested the $13,096 he was saving in mortgage payments since his house was

---

[9] $27,500 - $13,096 = $14,404

paid off (for a total of $38,096 in the first year, reinvested every year thereafter). In the last option, Mike assumed Lenny had loan payments to make, but nets a return of 11% on the borrowed $250,000 value of the house.

If Lenny didn't change his situation, the appreciation of the paid off house plus the invested mortgage payments will give him $365,299 in gains over the seven years. However, if Lenny used the equity in his house for an investment loan, Lenny will have more than $1 million in value, even after subtracting the inflation.

Teaching Lenny this strategy led Mike into narrowing down the options of what to do with a home, the mortgage, and the money locked into it:

1) Pay off the mortgage, own house outright, and never borrow against the equity (the common middle class trap);

ATM?

Automated Teller Machine: a machine that dispenses money at the push of a button using a bank card.

2) Pay off the mortgage, then use the house as collateral for a loan and spend the borrowed money directly (the ATM model);

3) Pay down the mortgage, then use the house as collateral for a loan, invest this re-borrowed money, and then reinvest and/or spend the return on the investment (the millionaire model).

Option (1) is like using the home like a giant piggy bank. Although it is worth a lot of money, the equity trapped in the house is growing at the rate of inflation, which Mike already determined to be an unacceptable return. Option (1) also has to take into the account the potential millions that will vanish in terms of lost investment opportunity. The paid-off home in option (1) can't be used to pay bills, so Mike's family could literally starve to death this way. If he needed the money trapped in his house for anything, with this strategy he'd have to sell the house to access the money. If he sells the house, not only would he have the same amount of purchasing power as he had when he first got the home, he now needs to look for a place to live which will require his capital to be used again. He'll either have to downsize or move to a lower cost neighbourhood. Indeed, option (1) is a very bad option. To Mike this was not even worthy of considering a strategy – it's an option for people who have no strategy.

Option 1 – Pay off the house

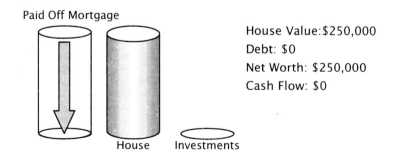

Paid Off Mortgage

House Value:$250,000
Debt: $0
Net Worth: $250,000
Cash Flow: $0

House   Investments

Option (2) wasn't any better. Mike saw this option being used by middle class families who were paying off the house, but needed the money, and didn't want to sell their house or move. Many times this is referred to as people treating their homes like a bank ATM (Automated Teller Machine), withdrawing the money from their house equity to spend on anything from vacations to children's education, or whatever they needed money for at the time. Samantha and Harry used it to remodel their kitchen. If they keep spending their house equity on more consumer items, they would end up back where they started when they first got the house decades earlier. They would have no investments and a full mortgage to pay again. They end up paying the interest all over once more, and the value of the house is just keeping up with inflation. The homeowner ends up paying double the cost of interest for a giant piggy bank that is empty, and no investments for retirement. Option (2) is worse than option (1).

> **Option 2:**
>
> *Worse than option 1.*

Option 2 - Pay off the house so we can use it like an ATM

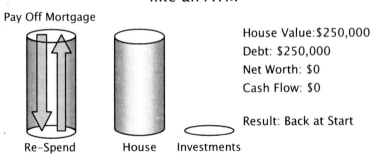

Pay Off Mortgage

Re-Spend   House   Investments

House Value: $250,000
Debt: $250,000
Net Worth: $0
Cash Flow: $0

Result: Back at Start

Mike figured out that option (3) is the best, and it's the model Mike used to build his wealth. As we'll soon see, this option provides the most capital, gets the most tax back, places money in better rates of return, and provides cash flow to pay the bills. This is the option Mike showed to Lenny.

Option 3 – Pay off the house, re-spend the borrowed money on investments!

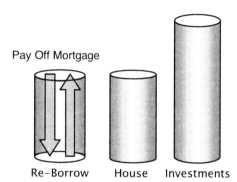

Pay Off Mortgage

Re-Borrow   House   Investments

Investment Value: $350,000
House Value: $250,000
Debt: $250,000
Net Worth: $100,000
Cash Flow: $27,500

Result: Cash in Pocket and increasing net worth

Conversely, option (3) provided money for Mike to invest in places that returned income every month. That money could be used to do anything from paying bills to reducing the mortgage (thus providing more equity to borrow), to just enjoying life. With this structure, Mike could see he would have more money every month. If Mike lost his job, a paid off house doesn't do him any good – but having this capital churning out cash every month provided him with a backup plan to prepare for the bad times and extra income in the good times.

We will see the details of exactly *how* Mike made this work in the next chapter, *Mike's Magnificent Mortgage Move.*

SUMMARY

Mike concluded that all of the house price boosting factors today have been nearly maxed out, leaving wages as the only real factor that keeps prices increasing. All else being equal, the public will only be able to afford bigger mortgages as their wages increase. Essentially, this limits an investment in a personal home to grow with the current rate of inflation. Since inflation means there are more dollars but they are worth less over time, an investment in a personal home is not an investment at all.

Even if the price of the house was able to surpass the rate of inflation, any real return was diminished by interest, lost opportunity, other upkeep costs, and market risk. Thus, the overall real rate of return is very poor and usually negative making the home a consumer item, not an investment. Even if Mike got a great return on his house like Harry and Samantha, he couldn't spend the bricks, mortar, and shingles that made up the value of his house. This is why Mike believed it was necessary to restructure his home finances to position himself better for financial freedom, just like his wealthy mentors have been doing for years.

The good news was that Mike now understood how a personal home was a trap. He also knew he could spring the trap by borrowing against it to acquire real assets. This was the best of both worlds. Mike got to keep both the appreciation of the house value as well as the investments. A fully re-borrowed home loan for investment purposes was excellent leverage, more liquid, and much safer than having just a mortgage. So as long as he followed his wealthy mentors and moved his mortgage into a better investment, he was on the road to success.

MIKE'S MAGNIFICENT MORTGAGE MOVE

"Those who understand compound interest, collect it. Those who don't, pay it."

- Albert Einstein
Theoretical physicist (1879 – 1955)

BREAKING THE PIGGY BANK

Many people move houses. But Mike was now convinced he had to move his mortgage. Since Mike didn't consider his home to be a good investment any more, what he had to do was take money out of this hungry piggy bank and put it to work. He was determined to turn his lost opportunity into seized opportunity. To do so, he first determined the numbers he had to work with. How much money was in his piggy bank?

THE MIDDLE CLASS WEALTH FOUNTAIN

As Mike built this system using middle class traps to create an abundance of wealth, he envisioned an analogy of a middle class wealth fountain. In this wealth fountain, Mike could see the money flowing from one part of the fountain to another, with each bucket along the way serving a different purpose.

Using his middle class wealth fountain analogy, the first stage was the home equity bucket. Mike determined that each of the buckets in the fountain have a certain capacity, which is the amount of capital allocated to that part of the system. In order to size up the home equity stage in the fountain, Mike simply calculated the amount of equity he had in his home.

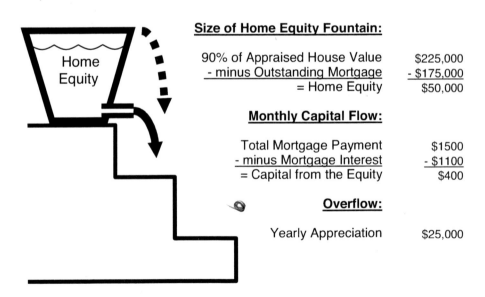

Size of Home Equity Fountain:

90% of Appraised House Value	$225,000
- minus Outstanding Mortgage	- $175,000
= Home Equity	$50,000

Monthly Capital Flow:

Total Mortgage Payment	$1500
- minus Mortgage Interest	- $1100
= Capital from the Equity	$400

Overflow:

Yearly Appreciation	$25,000

Mike purchased his house a few years ago for $225,000, but when he had the home appraised at current market prices it was valued at $250,000. His bankers told Mike that he needed to have 10% of the value of his house paid off before they would lend him any money using the house as collateral. Mike discovered that most lenders usually required between 10% to 25% equity to be kept in the house, and would lend out the other 75% to 90%. Mike found a lender that would lend him 90% of the value of the house, which meant he could borrow up to $225,000 against his $250,000 house. Since Mike had been making mortgage payments for a few years, his mortgage was down to $175,000, which meant he could pull out $50,000 as a loan. This was the difference between the 90% value of his house and the remaining mortgage ($225,000 - $175,000). This was the size of his home equity bucket.

Mike's banker set up a second account, called a "Home Equity Line of Credit" (HELOC). Now Mike had two accounts that used his house as collateral: 1) His shrinking original mortgage, and 2) This new HELOC.

Setting the HELOC Stage

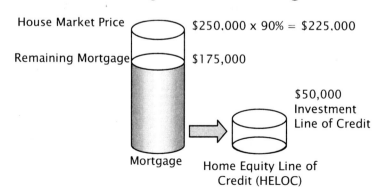

House Market Price — $250,000 x 90% = $225,000

Remaining Mortgage — $175,000

$50,000 Investment Line of Credit

Mortgage

Home Equity Line of Credit (HELOC)

Using this HELOC, Mike was now able to begin shifting money out of his house, and into other assets that would give him a better rate of return on his money.

HOW TO MAKE THE SHIFT

Instead of heading toward a paid-off house, Mike wanted to build up a big safe portfolio outside of his home and profit from much higher rates of return. The first thing he did was use the value of his house to re-borrow the maximum the bank would lend him right away, $50,000. Once this initial lump sum was withdrawn and invested, every time he made another mortgage payment, it increased the equity in his house by a few hundred dollars. Using this increased equity as more collateral, he would immediately use the HELOC account to borrow back the amount of principle he just paid down, and then make another investment. Every month he made a mortgage payment, and every month he was able to take out more equity from his home and invest it.

Making the Shift

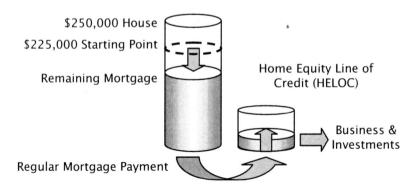

$250,000 House
$225,000 Starting Point
Remaining Mortgage
Home Equity Line of Credit (HELOC)
Business & Investments
Regular Mortgage Payment

Mike was essentially converting his mortgage debt in one account into investment debt in the other account on a regular basis. The overall amount of debt stayed the same, but its purpose and characteristics changed. We'll take a look at where Mike put this money in later chapters on business and investments. For now, let's just take a look at the benefits of doing this shuffle.

CAPITAL IS "DISCOVERED" FOR INVESTMENTS

Initially, Mike's problem was by the time he paid his bills, his mortgage and his taxes, he had no money left to invest. However, he now had a sizeable lump sum to invest and every time he paid against his mortgage, he had more again. He had to make his mortgage payments in order to live in his house anyway, but now he was using that capital to invest – twice! Now with his new dual account set-up, each time he made a mortgage payment, he freed up more credit. With this new credit he was able to take out the same amount of principle he paid down as a business or investment loan. Like magic, he found a source of funds without having to change his budget one cent.

After a few months of mortgage payments, Mike's mortgage was continuously being converted into a business loan and an investment loan. Mike learned that a business or investment loan carries many more benefits than a mortgage.

INTEREST BECOMES DEDUCTIBLE IN CANADA

Unlike his co-workers at the company's American sister office in Seattle, Mike couldn't automatically deduct his mortgage interest from his taxes in Canada. However, he could deduct loan interest used to make income from business and investments. So this move allowed Mike as a Canadian to start deducting massive amounts of interest on his tax returns, since his new HELOC was a tax-deductible expense. Instead of the interest *remaining* deductible as it was for Americans, it *became* deductible for Mike as a Canadian.

How much tax was did this translate into? Mike was paying six percent interest on his original $225,000 mortgage which equated to $13,500 per year. At Mike's tax bracket, writing off this interest would save him over $5,000 in income tax each year.

GETTING PERPETUAL INTEREST DEDUCTIONS

Since Mike was converting his mortgage debt into business and investment debt, he could potentially keep deducting the interest from his taxes for the rest of his tax life. Mike's plan was to always keep this debt going, to always keep the tax deduction and investment income coming into his pocket.

Keeping his debt going meant that his total outstanding debt and interest payable would be constant, whereas mortgage debt and interest payments usually decrease over time. The decreasing mortgage interest gets converted into constantly deductible investment interest.

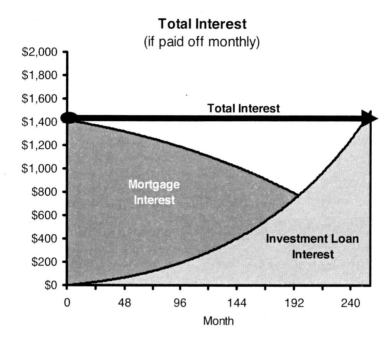

Now Mike was paying the same amount of interest in the tenth year as he was in the first year. It was alright with Mike that he kept paying interest on an ongoing basis, because his investments were making a higher rate of return than the interest he was paying, so it was positive leverage. Though it was counter to everything he had been told growing up, he realized that the more debt he had, the more money he made because of this positive leverage.

positive leverage

Positive Leverage
Cost < Gain

Since Mike could re-borrow the money at 6% and he could conservatively make at least 17% on his money in millionaire style investments, such as the apartment complex he showed Lenny, it was a good move as his net return was 11%. Mike compared this to if he had bought a bigger house that was going to appreciate at an average rate of 5% per year. In that case, his six percent mortgage interest loses him money every month. While he was initially concerned about borrowing to invest, now that he understood he was already borrowing to invest in his home, it didn't seem nearly as scary.

Mike then came to an interesting dilemma: to pay, or not to pay? If he paid off the interest on the investment loan each month, his total debt would be steady – his total debt would equal the starting amount he borrowed for his house: the original $225,000. The total amount of debt and interest he owed would look like a flat line.

But why would Mike pay off a 6% interest rate, when he could easily reinvest this money to earn at least 17% or more? His banker agreed to "capitalize the interest" for him. What this meant was that the bank simply added the interest onto the debt he already owed. Instead of being a steady flat line of debt, it slowly increased over time. Alternatively, if capitalization wasn't an option at his bank, Mike could have simply paid the interest on the HELOC using another loan or line of credit.

Total Interest
(if allowed to accumulate)

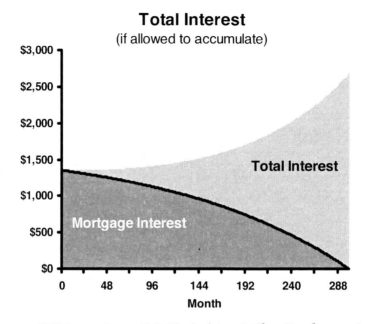

"Wait a minute!" Mike's friend Charlie shouted, as Mike was explaining the system to him. "You mean I'm going to pay *more* money in interest, on purpose?!"

"Absolutely!" Mike shouted back to him. Mike showed Charlie that the money he was going to make far outweighed the extra interest he owed each month. The interest he was paying compounded against him at 6%, and his investments compounded in his favour at 17%. Besides, Mike reminded him that he was paying 6% interest on a mortgage for a house that was appreciating at 5%, and already turning a loss of 1 percent each year. He was also losing another large amount of money in lost investment opportunity on any money that was locked in his house as equity. Once Charlie realized that he was already losing money, he became much more open to the idea of putting his money to work for him, instead of against him.

Mike explained to Charlie that negative leverage is often dubbed as the other side of the double-edged blade of borrowing money to invest. The danger lies when the investment makes less than the cost of the loan. Since house prices rise with inflation, and interest rates usually exceed published inflation rates, a home is almost always doomed to be negative leverage.

Negative Leverage

Costing 6% Interest > Gain 5% Appreciation
(plus)
17% in Lost Investment Opportunity > 5% Appreciation

Because Mike could calculate the minimum return he was going to get on his investment, it was well worth paying the little bit extra interest for the substantial returns he was going to make. When the investment returns are higher than the interest costs, the return on investment more than pays for the additional cost of interest.

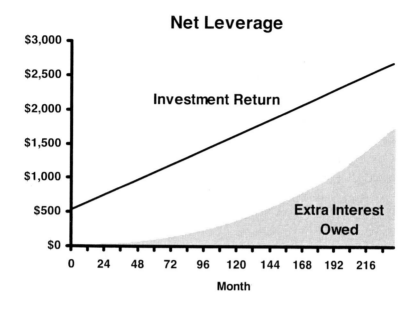

While Mike felt comfortable with this, he explained to Charlie he had options. If Charlie didn't like owing the extra interest, he could always take a little bit from his return and pay the extra interest off. If he did this however, he would have less capital to invest and his returns would be lower. The choice was ultimately determined by Charlie's comfort level.

THE YEAR BY YEAR PLAY

Even though Mike was re-borrowing the equity stored in his house, he still maintained rights to the value of the appreciation on that house. In other words, any gains from the increase in price were still his to keep. The difference between the selling price and the total loan owing remained as his collateral to either cash out upon selling it, or re-borrow while he lived in it.

After one year of 5% appreciation on his $250,000 home, Mike gained $12,500 in equity. In addition to re-borrowing the principle portion of his monthly mortgage *payments*, he also borrowed this *appreciation* on the house.

This gave him an added bonus, as he paid a low interest rate for this loan he could use it to gain a higher rate of return. Mike intended to have his home reappraised every few years, so that he could increase the amount of money he could borrow against his home as it increased in price.

> *Appreciation* constantly adds to the amountof capital that can be pulled out of the house.

HOW THE MORTGAGE STORY ENDS

Much like a Walt Disney story, Mike could see that his mortgage story was destined to have a "happily ever after" type ending. After years of making the usual mortgage payments, continually deducting thousands of dollars in interest from his taxes, and building a massive portfolio, Mike could foresee that his situation would look like this:

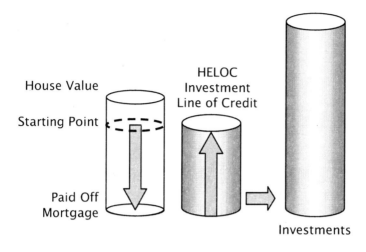

Technically, his house was paid for because the mortgage was gone. It had been replaced by a business and investment loan, secured by the house. If Mike ever wanted to pay off this debt, then all he would have to do is close some investments and write a cheque to pay back the loan. He would still have money left over in his investment accounts.

Now Mike had options if he needed money, he wouldn't *have to* sell his house if he didn't want to. He also could live off the returns his investments were making him. Mike positioned himself for security and independence.

Using only the safely invested house equity and associated tax benefits, Mike's investment values were structured to escalate substantially.

				HELOC Loan	Investment
		House Value	Mortgage	Amount	Value
Start		$250,000	$175,000	$50,000	$50,000
Year	1	$265,000	$164,006	$74,494	$82,689
Year	2	$280,900	$152,461	$100,349	$120,483
Year	3	$297,754	$140,340	$127,639	$164,028
Year	4	$315,619	$127,613	$156,445	$214,046
Year	5	$334,556	$114,249	$186,852	$271,343
Year	6	$354,630	$100,217	$218,950	$336,819
Year	7	$375,908	$85,483	$252,834	$411,480
Year	8	$398,462	$70,013	$288,603	$496,447
Year	9	$422,370	$53,769	$326,364	$592,970
Year	10	$447,712	$36,713	$366,228	$702,446
Year	11	$474,575	$18,804	$408,313	$826,430
Year	12	$503,049	$0	$452,744	$966,656
Year	13	$533,232	$0	$479,909	**$1,103,141**

Assumptions

Home Appreciation	6%
Net Investment Return	11%

Not only could Mike see he'd be able to keep deducting the interest paid from his taxes, he could leverage the capital into better investments than his house. His escape from the mortgage trap would solve his lack of capital and cash flow in a few ways:

1. He now would have a source of massive capital through accessing his home equity.

2. He would increase his tax efficiency for the rest of his tax life.

3. He could start a chain of investments to create usable cash flow.

FREE YOUR MIND, AND THE CASH WILL FOLLOW

Many of Mike's friends still couldn't believe what he was doing. They thought it was crazy to borrow to invest, despite the great returns Mike was getting with his safe strategies. In fact, Mike was in a safer position than his peers, because he had his house paid off and he had investments paying him passive income. Mike began to understand that the feeling of safety is a matter of perspective and emotion, not a matter of logic.

To help his friends understand why it was not crazy for him to borrow to invest, he asked them one simple question: "Would you take out a loan to buy a car?" The answer was invariably, "yes." Mike saw that they had no problem borrowing large sums of money to buy a car that is guaranteed to go down in value, but they couldn't grasp the concept of borrowing the same amount of money to buy an asset that would go up in value. "Besides," as he kept explaining to them, "they were already borrowing to invest – in their house – and losing money at it!"

Mike knew that these were facts, as numbers don't lie. Any apprehension was caused purely by psychology and emotion. Mike suggested that they may not be "getting it" because their mental financial blueprint was not wired for wealth. In other words, they couldn't psychologically perceive themselves as making lots of money or being rich. Or perhaps they thought that it was not important to think about their own wealth.

Mike highly recommended books such as Napoleon Hill's classic *Think and Grow Rich* and the more modern *Secrets of the Millionaire Mind* by T. Harv Eker to help them reshape their non-supportive thought patterns about money. Eker's book even included a free 3-day workshop on how to rewire psychological beliefs for wealth. Believe it or not, this change in mentality can make a huge difference in a person's success. Think about all the people with drained inheritances or lottery winnings. They obviously didn't have a physical problem getting the money, they had a mental problem keeping it!

SUMMARY

A paid-off home isn't an asset, as it doesn't pay the bills. It isn't a great investment either, and it can even be a negative leverage purchase with a negative return on investment. Mike's new plan was to never have the house paid off, as the equity needed to be re-borrowed and put elsewhere.

Instead of building up this massive equity in his home, Mike began converting the mortgage debt into business and investment debt. He did this by opening a second account – a Home Equity Line of Credit (HELOC) – and replaced his mortgage with it. This liberated a great amount of capital that was locked into a forced savings account – his home. Investing his newly freed forced savings created a portfolio that did pay the bills. This let Mike escape the trap of having to spend the re-borrowed money from his house when he needed it, which would have put him back at square one.

As a Canadian, converting his mortgage debt into business and investment debt allowed Mike to deduct the interest he paid from his income taxes. These interest deductions allowed Mike to pay less tax in the long run, to the tune of thousands of dollars. Mike looked forward to receiving big tax refunds at the end of every year.

Finally, Mike would never be forced to sell his home if he didn't want to, as his investments would be able to cover the cost of the loan. If the loan needed repayment, the investments can be liquidated and the loan repaid. The difference is literally millions of dollars added to Mike's asset base, simply from restructuring his mortgage.

Mike discovered that placing this money in vehicles that generate capital and create passive income for him would be a critical step in escaping the middle class job trap.

WHAT YOUR BOSS ISN'T TELLING YOU

"I would rather earn 1% off a 100 people's efforts than 100% of my own efforts."

- John Paul Getty
American oil man and industrialist (1892 - 1976)

WAYS OF CREATING CAPITAL

At this point in the journey, Mike was still working at his job. This used to be his only available source of capital and income.

But like the fly that inspired his journey, he realized he needed to step backwards to take a look at the big picture. Since he was planning an escape from the middle class norms, he would eventually end up in unknown financial territory. What did this territory look like, and how did people who lived there make their money if they weren't working?

Mike figured that he had two basic ways of creating capital: he could earn and save it through trading time for money working at his job, or he could create it through trading value for profits through a business. He knew his salary had an upper limit to the amount that he could earn – his boss would only pay him so much. However, a business theoretically had no limit on the amount of profits it could make – it's just a matter of more sales. A business could either be one he was running, or someone else's business in which he had invested. Since those who are financially free aren't working, Mike's mentors pointed out they derive their income from these investment and business profits.

THE SECRET TO BECOMING FINANCIALLY FREE

After reading a few wealth generation books such as Robert Kiyosaki's *Cash Flow Quadrant*, Mike began to validate that he needed this something called "passive income" to become financially free.

Passive Income: *Cash flow that keeps being paid to you whether you're actively working for it or not. Also known as pyjama money – if you were lying around in your pyjamas doing nothing, this money would still be flowing into your bank account.*

In fact, Mike needed enough passive income to cover all his expenses in order to stop working at his job and maintain his desired lifestyle.

This concept of passive income was fairly new to Mike, as it's not something that the school system taught him. One of his goals when he started this journey was to become a millionaire. However, if his million dollars was earning him five percent interest, this would only provide him with an income of $50,000 per year – less than he was making now working as an engineer!

Mike began to realize that if he was invested in a business that paid him $50,000 a year in passive income, this is equivalent to a million dollar portfolio paying him five percent per year. If his business paid him $100,000 per year, this would be the same as his million dollar portfolio paying him interest of 10% per year. So Mike began to think in terms of his monthly cash flow, rather than in terms of net worth. He didn't necessarily need to shoot for the million dollar mark as much as he needed business and investment vehicles to pay him his desired monthly cash flow.

Mike set a three phase goal for his passive income levels:

1. Meet his current minimum expenses
2. Match his current salary
3. Double his current salary

What he also didn't know before his escape was that there are business models available with passive income designed right into the business. The business creators do this purposefully, so that the owner can eventually sit back and cash the cheques after all of the initial work and setup was done. With this model, the business owner and the investor essentially have the same role in the end – sit back and collect the income. The difference being that the business owner works at the business at first, whereas the investor was passive since the beginning of the investment.

After this research, Mike planned to build a business and investment portfolio with his capital that would pay him this regular cash flow. But first, he couldn't resist trying to find out why it was that he didn't know about these opportunities sooner.

WHO DID SOCIETY TURN YOU INTO?

Why had Mike not known about building a passive income portfolio before he met his mentors? If he knew this earlier, he would have started working on building up his passive income right after school – or maybe even sooner. Instead, he spent most of his time and effort either working at, or looking for a job that didn't provide him with any passive income.

Mike found that he was educated to get a job paying a wage, and then live month to month off that wage (and credit card debt of course). But, if Mike lost that job he'd be in trouble because then his income also stops. By having passive income, Mike wouldn't have to worry about losing his job. In fact, he figured he wouldn't even really need life insurance if he had this passive income, because passive income wasn't dependent on him living for it to pay him. Even better, he could do whatever he wanted to do with his time once he reached that point, because every minute of his life would belong to him, not his boss.

By learning more about creating passive business income, he was gradually becoming aware that society at large had very little to teach him about making money, but a great deal to show him about how to spend his money. If he was going to learn, he would have to put himself through school again. But this was a different kind of school – a self-motivated school – as no regular schoolteacher was going to take him by the hand and show him how to become financially free.

GREAT-GRANDPA, WHY ARE YOU STILL WORKING?

Mike realized that building a passive income portfolio, including from his own business and other peoples' businesses, was the only way for him to become financially free or retire. He observed many people were working longer into their old age, simply because they weren't structuring their finances to support them properly. They were trying to build a big pile of money, but had no steady passive cash flow coming from it. Having the house paid off was a great example of that mentality. People like Samantha and Harry may have that million-dollar home but they'll still be living month-to-month off their salary from a job that they hate. They might have some small savings or a nest egg, but rarely was that nest egg paying them income on a monthly or quarterly basis. A situation that is even worse is some people are in the habit of living month-to-month and have no assets and no plan at all. Either way, rarely did Mike observe the typical middle class investor with any regular substantial income from investments. Having no passive income and no assets translates into a lifetime of working.

Mike wanted to exceed his current salary with passive income, as he didn't want to work until age 65 or 75, live on any less money, or lower his standard of living. Many financial advisers had told Mike that he could plan to retire with less money. The common wisdom was that if the house is paid off, you need less money to live. When Mike asked what would happen if he needed to re-borrow the money locked in the house to access the cash, or about inflation eating away at his money, or even why he should intend to spend less money when he had more free time on his hands, there were few answers that satisfied him. Mike had found that we don't need less money to become "retired", we need more – and it needs to be in the form

What Mike meant by "work" was any task that came from **external motivation**. When someone is financially free, they are still going to contribute to society, but it will be a contribution of what they *enjoy* doing instead of what they *have to* do – **internal motivation**. If you like what you do, you'll never "work" another day in your life.

of passive income, not from a job. A job is like a financial prison.

WORK VERSUS PRISON

One day Mike got a joke email that put everything in perspective for him. It was entitled "Work vs. Prison."

Prison	Work
You spend the majority of your time in a 10 x 10 cell.	You spend the majority of your time in an 8 x 8 cubicle.
You get three meals a day, fully paid for.	You get a break for one meal, and you have to pay for it.
You get time off for good behaviour.	You get more work for good behaviour.
The guard locks, unlocks, and opens all the doors for you.	You often carry a security card and open all the doors yourself.
You can watch TV and play games.	You could get fired for watching TV and playing games.
You get your own toilet.	You share the toilet with other people who pee on the seat.
They allow your family and friends to visit.	You aren't supposed to speak to your family.
The taxpayers pay all expenses with no work required.	You pay all your expenses to go to work, and they deduct taxes from your salary to pay for prisoners.
You spend most of your life inside bars wanting to get out.	You spend most of your time wanting to get out to go inside bars.

Even though it was a joke it did put things into perspective. After all, Mike found if we need money and if the only way we know how to get money is a paycheque, we are essentially chained to the job. Habits are hard to break, and the longer humans repeat something, the deeper the habit becomes ingrained. The deeper the habit, the harder it is to escape. The longer we rely on a paycheque instead of passive income, the harder the escape becomes psychologically.

We should be designing our financial lives to escape dependence on a job, and replace it with independence. Passive income, as Mike found, is the key to escape the job trap.

HOW TO LIVE A LONGER LIFE

Mike didn't want to wait until he was a senior citizen to "retire". He always thought life was too short to wait that long to have his days to himself to do whatever he wanted to do – instead of giving his days to his boss. After all, we're only on this earth for a limited number of days, and Mike wanted to make the most of it. He wanted to decide what he was trading his life for.

He once read an article about how Boeing's pension plan had conducted a study of the relationship between how long people work compared to how long they live. The study was based on the number of pension cheques sent to retirees of Boeing Aerospace. Research indicated that for people who retired at the age of 55, their average life span was 86; whereas for people who retired at the age of 65, their average life span was 66.8 years. An important conclusion from this study was that for every year worked beyond age 55, Mike expected to lose two years of his life span. Mike certainly did not need to work longer to die earlier, a probable fate that was determined by the good folks at Boeing.

But Mike's goal wasn't to retire even as "early" as 55 – he wanted to become financially free well before then. More specifically, he wanted to do it using everyday things available to the middle class. He already had set himself up, by turning his mortgage trap into a vehicle for investment income. Using that investment income to escape the job trap was the second step.

SUMMARY

Society doesn't educate us about investing for passive income or creating our own business profits. The passive income that sets us free comes from these businesses and investments, not a job. The benefits of passive income are huge, including freedom, happiness, and longevity in life. Mike decided not to plan to be broke in retirement and die early. He decided to retire early and profitably. And the first step was setting up his own passive income in the form of a home-based business.

MINDING YOUR OWN BUSINESS

> *"Profits are better than wages. Wages make you a living, which is fine. Profits can make you a fortune, which is super fine."*
>
> *- Jim Rohn*
> Business Philosopher, Motivator and Trainer

FUNDING IS SECURED – NOW WHAT?

Mike knew that passive income could come from either investments or from his own business. Where was the best place to put his capital first? What had the priority? As it turned out, there was no contest.

Mike's ultimate goal was to become financially free and to become very wealthy. The problem of finding capital had been solved by converting his mortgage debt into investment debt, giving him a huge source of funds to invest. Now the issue was where to invest it.

Mike had two basic options of where to invest this newly found capital:

1. Invest it in his own business
2. Invest it in someone else's business

There were many factors to consider for each option, but the main items that Mike considered were capital limitations, tax considerations and return limitations.

Mike was limited how much he could buy from someone else by the amount of capital he could access. However, Mike found that he could start a business for himself with very little money and leverage this into a magnified amount of benefits. Therefore, at this stage his own business had the upper hand.

From a tax perspective, his own business was a much better place for his capital. He learned from talking to his tax professionals that under current income tax regulations, if he invested the capital into someone else's business (in other words, if Mike bought a conventional investment product like a stock, bond, or mutual fund), that he could only deduct the interest if that investment could produce him income. However, if he invested the money in his own business in the form of a business loan, the interest became a business expense and could be deducted from his total income right away – even before he made any income.

This meant that he could reduce the taxes he paid on his working salary by simply deducting the interest on his business loan. In addition to the business loan interest, Mike would be able to start deducting other business expenses from his taxes as well. For instance, he could deduct his vehicle, travel, furniture, office supplies, and telephone expenses, among other things.

Mike determined from a tax perspective it was definitely better to set up his own business first rather than investing in someone else's. And though Mike didn't know it at the time, when he invested in his home business first, he also liberated capital for other purposes in addition to reducing his taxes – all before he made his first profit.

Finally, Mike reasoned that he could add something extra to his own business that he couldn't add to his investments: sweat equity. In other words, Mike could use his own spare time and effort to build the business. He could use evenings and weekends to add value and sales to

Sweat Equity: Time and effort Mike puts into the business.

his business. Any profits generated from this sweat equity on his part would be put directly into his own pocket. He just couldn't add his efforts to his investments in the same way. In the beginning when his capital was low, but his time, effort, and determination were high, this sweat equity turned into extra capital, which Mike could use to invest.

It was a slam-dunk. Investing in his own business was better on all three counts. Finally, for leverage reasons it was also better for Mike to boost his tax refund first before investing the money. Mike had to choose between investing $100, or using the same $100 to get $200 in tax back, he figured the best order was to get the taxes back first. He could then use the $200 from his tax refund to fund his investment – twice as much as he had originally.

WHY BUSINESSES PAY LESS TAX

Mike was obligated to pay taxes. However, he found that by setting up a personal business, he changed the way he was taxed. As it turned out, that made a huge difference. He could immediately see why his new wealthy friends all had private businesses.

Using the business structure was a key component to this strategy. Mike took a look at the difference between how individuals are taxed, and how businesses are taxed:

Individual	Business
Income – Tax	Revenue – Expenses
=	=
Disposable Income	Taxable Profits

Mike noticed how individuals get taxed on the income right away, and then use the rest as disposable income. However, businesses subtract the expenses first, and then only pay taxes on the remaining profit. For Mike it was obvious that the ideal situation was to pay the least amount of tax, therefore the business model was much more appealing than being taxed as an individual. The key was for Mike to convert himself into a business – specifically a sole proprietorship – in order to be able to start subtracting expenses first from his personal wages, and then get taxed on the rest. The expenses that are subtracted from personal revenues (wages) are called "deductions."

Deductions: Mike subtracted the money he spent in his business from his salary, reducing the tax he owed.

Types of Business Structures

Sole Proprietor Business: Revenues and expenses fall under Mike personally

Partnership: Revenues and expenses divides between partners

Corporation: Revenues and expenses accounted for as a separate entity from Mike

Since Mike was paying 25 percent in his top income tax bracket, he thought of it as getting a 25 percent discount on everything he bought that was a tax-deductible business expense. The more expenses he deducted, the more tax he saved.

CHANGING THE SPENDING PERSPECTIVE

As Mike became aware of these great home business tax benefits, it was time to take action and get into business for himself. Since he was new at this and wanted to start small, he decided that a part-time, home based business was the way to go. With this approach, he would be able to stop spending some of his money as personal expenses, and start spending that money as business expenses. In some cases, he would use a certain percentage of the expense for business, and so he would be able to deduct that portion of the cost as a business expense. When he used his car 30% of the time for business, he deducted 30% of those as business expenses.

Mike started to keep track of when, where, and with who he was doing business. He started keeping track of the mileage on his car, telephone and internet use, and pretty much anything else he was using for business. Soon, he had quite a file folder on his previous personal expenses that were now business expenses.

He also began to change his perspective on how he got his personal affairs done. He was still driving the same car, but now he was using it more and more for business than for personal reasons. Instead of making a personal trip, he would simply take care of his personal affairs during a business trip. For example, instead of making a special trip to go out and get bread for his family, he would pick the bread up on the way home from a business outing. Now Mike's trip wasn't made for personal reasons, it was made for business reasons. The fact that he also happened to get some personal items taken care of at the same time was just a bonus.

As Mike kept track of the money he was spending on all of his expenses, he started to deduct these expenses from the salary he was making. Since he was now running his life as a business, the portion of the money he spent on business expenses wasn't taxed. This saved him massive amounts of taxes, giving him more capital to use in his wealth strategies.

Mike talked a lot with his tax professional and began learning more about the world of business expenses. After working with his tax advisor to integrate the tax deduction system into his life, he was streamlined for tax deductions throughout his financial dealings.

Originally, Mike didn't have much money to fund any sort of business activity. However many of his business expenses came from money he was already spending. He was already spending money on a car. He was already paying for home office equipment. He already spent money on travel. He already paid a phone bill. Only now that he was running a life based on a business, he started to deduct as many expenses as he could justify. In essence, he started doing business in many aspects of his life – and many aspects of his spending became deductible from his taxes.

Mike learned that tax deductions are all about creative justification. As long as he could realistically justify it as a business expense, it was in fact a business expense. Although he couldn't justify *all* of his expenses to be business, the large number he did deduct was well worth it. Because of the nature of the business he eventually chose, he was almost always in a position to conduct his business affairs. Whether it was to make a sale or to gain a business partner, he was always looking for the opportunity to engage in some sort of business activity. He even wrote a company dress standard and uniform policy into his business plan, so that he could deduct clothing expenses. His creative justification allowed him to write off everything from suits when meeting with bankers, to jeans when meeting with farmers.

CORE BUSINESS COSTS

Even though many of Mike's new business expenses were already being spent as personal expenses before he started his business, there were some additional items he had to buy in order to run the business. Mike referred to these as **core costs** of doing business, and included items such as business supplies, advertising, business cards and flyers. These are expenses that he wouldn't have if he didn't have the business. Mike had to have core costs, but he also kept them to a minimum. Mike added the core costs to his total expenses he was deducting from his taxes.

Total Deductible Expense Composition

Existing	Previous personal expenses Mike converted into business expenses
+ Core	Extra money Mike spent to do business
= Total Expenses	Total deductible business expenses

Core costs are the cost of doing business. They allowed Mike access to profits, as well as justify being in business and write-off business expenses. If Mike didn't have any core costs, and also didn't have any profits, the tax authorities may question whether Mike actually had a business or not. Core costs were part of Mike's proof that he had a "Reasonable Expectation of Profit." After all, why would Mike buy business cards if he didn't expect them to help him make a profit?

Get receipt for $1,000 for buying DKs + SB! subscription

The revenue that the business made directly offset Mike's core costs. For example, when Mike spent $100 on core costs, but made $100 in revenue, they cancelled each other out and any other expenses didn't cost Mike anything "out of pocket". However, Mike still deducted the non-core expenses from his taxes and got the tax back. Since the business paid for itself, Mike effectively got the deductions "for free," as the business wasn't costing him anything directly.

However, Mike didn't know when his business was going to start generating revenue, so he liked to base everything on the assumption that it wasn't profitable yet. This way, he knew that even if the business wasn't making a profit yet, he would still be getting a good return on his capital.

At first Mike based his return on investment according to his core business costs and what he got back in taxes. If it cost him $100 to get into business, and he was only getting $50 back in taxes, he needed to make a $50 profit in his business to stay in the black. However, if his business had a core cost of $100 and he calculated he would get back $200 in taxes – he knew he would double his investment costs even before he made his first sale. Since he could budget his expenses and estimate what percentage would be used for business, his net return on his business could be estimated well in advance of investing the money in his business.

The following is an example of Mike spending $100 on core business costs and what type of expenses he deducted from his job income. The figures are monthly figures.

Tax Table 1: What expenses are worth

Expense (Business Portion)	Deductible Amount
Business inventory supply & advertising ("core costs")	$100
Car expenses (mileage, maintenance, gas, etc.)	$150
Travel and gifts (monthly average)	$250
Meals and entertainment	$100
Office supplies (paper, pens, stationary)	$50
Furniture (average cost per month)	$50
Other equipment (computers, copiers, fax machines and scanners)	$50
Telephone charges (land line, long distance, cell phone for business)	$50
Insurance premiums (monthly average)	$50
Hiring his children as employees, babysitting	$50
Total Deductible Expenses	**= $900**
Total income tax refund @ 25% tax rate	x 25% = **$225**
Less core costs	- $100
Net cash increase	**= $125**
Return on investment (ROI)	*$125 / $100 =* **125% ROI**

Mike had never seen 125% return per year in any other investment he had ever made. What was even better is he could approximate in advance what he would make on this investment. When faced with the choice of whether to put $100 per month into a mutual fund for an unknown return or $100 per month into his own home-based business for an estimated return of 125%, the answer was plain to see. The numbers didn't lie.

After a little learning and practice, Mike was soon deducting a larger and larger portion of his total expenses as business expenses. This saved him a lot of tax in the long run. Below is his monthly before and after expense account:

Expenses Before Business	Expenses After Business
Personal: $1250	Personal: $450
Business: $0	Business: $900
Tax Owed: $337	Tax Owed: $112

Every time Mike spent money for business reasons, he would record on the back of the receipt what the expense was for and then file these receipts away for his tax professional.

HOW TO LIBERATE CASH FLOW

Mike was using his HELOC loan to pay for his business expenses. This was creating even more benefits for him in terms of generating available cash flow. Let's look at a simplified version of how Middle Class Mike used to pay his mortgage and his bills.

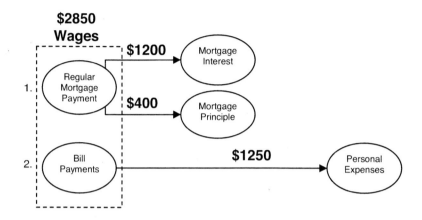

Before, Middle Class Mike used to take his wages and pay off $400 worth of mortgage principle and $1250 worth of personal expenses. His mortgage payments were always $1600 in total, and started out as $1200 in interest, $400 in principle.

Since Mike converted his life into a business life, many of these expenses were no longer non-deductible personal expenses. They were made into tax-deductible business expenses.

Mike's available credit was maxed out. This happens to people often: the bank says they won't lend them any more money, because their debt-to-income ratio is already too high. This simply meant that when Mike wanted to borrow another dollar, he had to pay down his mortgage principle by one dollar to create collateral for this borrowing ability. Then he could use

his paid principle as collateral for a business loan. He
then used this loan to pay for his
business expenses.

A re-advanceable mortgage
gave Mike the kind of
flexibility he needed with his
credit situation. It
automatically raised his
borrowing power every time
he paid his mortgage down.

The result of Mike using
his home equity to pay for his
business expenses was that he
had excess money left over from
the portion of his paycheque that used to pay these bills.
This freed up capital, called "liberated capital", and was
yet another advantage of using a home-based business
as a place to use investment capital.

Cash Flow Figure 1: The Early Years

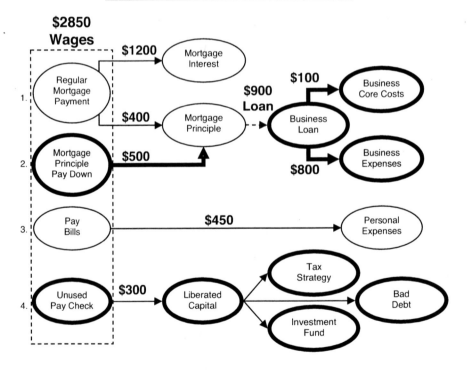

Mike still paid the same $1250 in total expenses ($800 Business + $450 Personal). However, instead of using cash from his wages to pay off the bills directly, Mike used some of the cash to pre-pay his mortgage principle. Since he doesn't pay down enough principle in his regular mortgage payment to build collateral for the entire loan, this additional principle payment in step 2 is necessary for him to increase his credit. This additional principle payment doesn't use up his entire pay cheque – he has money left over. Step 4 is where Mike used his liberated capital to fund the other portions of his strategy.

Liberated Capital: *Cash now available for use, because the bills are being paid from re-borrowed mortgage principle*

Mike could also calculate what his liberated capital would be each month by deducting the mortgage principle from the core costs. Since his expenses were increased slightly by core costs, his liberated capital was reduced slightly by the core costs.

Liberated Capital = Mortgage Principle - Core Costs

The good news was, as the mortgage principle was paid down the liberated capital increased. This was because Mike's core costs stayed the same over time, but the amount of his mortgage payment that went to principle increased every month.

Mike's liberated capital was cash, not borrowed money. Mike therefore thought it was best used for purposes where the interest on a loan wouldn't be tax-deductible anyway. Mike had three main possibilities of where to use his liberated cash flow: into a tax strategy, paying down bad debt, or paying into an investment. Again, the decision was made easy by running the numbers.

First, he made sure his tax strategy was fully funded. Next, Mike put this money towards converting more non-deductible "bad debt" into deductible "good debt." Bad debt was debt that charges interest that Mike couldn't deduct from his taxes or debt that didn't pay him any passive income. In Canada, a mortgage is actually bad debt as it's not tax deductible and doesn't pay any income. The idea was for Mike to convert this bad debt into good debt. Just like in the mortgage move, the bad debt is paid down, and a business or investment loan replaces it.

The final destination for any unused liberated capital was an investment. Mike only used cash for investments when his tax strategy was fully funded, all of his bad debt was converted to good debt, and he couldn't get any more investment loans. Mike always preferred to use borrowed money to invest, and use cash for anything that couldn't be deducted from his taxes, such as personal expenses.

As time passed, the principle component of his mortgage payments matched the amount he was taking out as a loan, and he didn't need to make pre-payments anymore. His $1600 mortgage payment was now broken into $900 for the principle and $700 for the interest.

Cash Flow Figure 2: The Middle Years

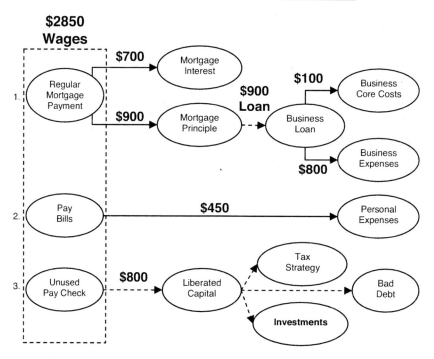

The less Mike had to pre-pay on the mortgage, the more liberated capital he could use elsewhere. Mike's liberated capital rose from $300 per month to $800.

As time passed, eventually Mike's principle component of his $1600 mortgage payment exceeded what he needed to run his business. Once this happened, he funnelled the excess capital directly into other strategies, such as investments.

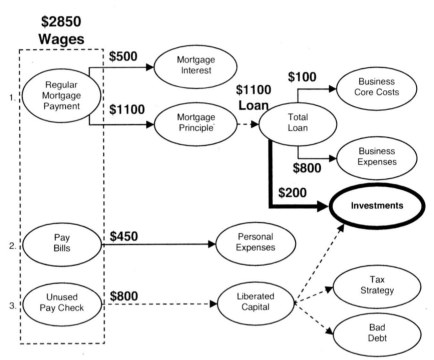

Cash Flow Figure 3: The Later Years

Mike used his liberated capital on a monthly basis, but had to wait until the end of the tax year to get his taxes back. He discussed with his accountant how he could get less tax withheld from his paycheque during the year, because he had these extra expenses. Although a large portion was still automatically taken off his salary, he did manage to lower it a little bit.

Let's see what Mike's average monthly situation looked like after he got his taxes back, using the numbers from the early years in Tax Table 1 and Cash Flow Figure #1:

	Monthly	Yearly
Tax Refund due to Business Expenses	$225 (average)	$2700
Liberated Capital	+ $300	$3600
Total Cash Flow	= $525 (average)	$6300

If Mike had decided to use his HELOC directly for investments, he would only have $4800 to use that first year ($400 monthly mortgage principle multiplied by 12 months). Since he boosted his tax return with the home-based business, Mike now had $6300 to use once he gets his taxes back – 31% more. Seeing as Mike's liberated capital went up every month, using this business loan strategy always made a better return for him than directly investing the money. This was the advantage of deductible business expenses.

Compare Capital Made Available:	
Invest Loan Directly	**Through Business Loan**
$400 (Principle Portion of Mortgage Payment) x 12 months = $4800 / year	$2700 Tax Refund + $3600 Liberated Capital = $6300 / year
Business Advantage = $1500 / year	

This advantage was gained even before he used the liberated capital, which increased his available capital further. As we will see in the later sections

Finishing the Income Tax Escape and *Investing like a Millionaire,* Mike put this liberated capital to good use and also made an excellent return. Mike ended up having much more than $6300 in his pocket to work with, all as a result of boosting his liberated capital.

Aside from the tax benefits and liberated capital there were even more good reasons for Mike to get into business for himself.

NO EXPERIENCE REQUIRED, APPLY WITHIN

At the outset, Mike figured he could make up what he lacked in capital by putting time and effort into his own business, and he called this "sweat equity."

He converted his personal time and effort into profits. The sweat equity Mike put into his business also gave him loads of business experience. Mike wanted to have experience in business, so that when it came time for him to become an investor, he would have knowledge about what to look for in a business to determine whether it was a good investment or not.

Based on discussions with his wealthy friends, Mike intended on investing directly in businesses because of the better returns and better security they said he would receive. He knew that he would need the business knowledge later, so he thought he had better start gaining the experience early in the game.

The great part was, unlike a job, he didn't need experience to start and start his own business. With his business, he was able to escape the catch-22 of the job trap where experience is needed to get the job, and a job is needed to gain experience.

All Mike had to do was apply himself and start his own business. "Apply within" had a new meaning to Mike. He appointed himself as the owner of his own business with zero resume and zero hassle.

WHAT WEALTHY PEOPLE DO FOR WORK

Many of the wealthy people – and more significantly, those who were financially free – who Mike read about owned their own business or invested in businesses.

It was important for Mike to structure himself the way they were structuring themselves, as they had obviously done well for themselves using this tactic. There was no need to reinvent the wheel, and these folks had already shown the most usual way to be wealthy was as a business owner.

Since Mike wasn't where his mentors were just yet, he viewed himself in transition – going from where he is to where he wanted to be.

HOW TO TRANSITION INTO WEALTH

Mike had still kept his job as his main source of income. He wasn't any sort of super-entrepreneur or mega investor yet, so he didn't figure it was viable to go out on his own until his passive income was well established. His plan was to work his business part time until he had the experience, expanded comfort level, and passive income to be able to leave his job. In the meantime, he would also build his business and investment portfolio.

Mike referred to this strategy as "transitioning to wealth" by learning and building his business and investments part-time. This reduced his risk and allowed Mike to keep paying the bills until he was financially free.

FINDING A GOOD BUSINESS

Mike had to conduct a search for a business. Obviously not all businesses were created equal, and some were better than others. Mike knew that there must be a business out there that perfectly suited his needs.

Mike sat down and created a list of factors he wanted to see in a business he would consider starting. Suddenly, he found that he was becoming a business analyst without even realizing it.

Mike's business criteria were:

❑ Passive income built into the business
❑ Ability to manage it part-time
❑ A business that is already operational
❑ Universal
❑ Flexible
❑ Business and sector that shows steady growth
❑ Low start-up costs
❑ Low operating costs
❑ Excellent profit margins
❑ National or global potential
❑ Large numbers of potential customers
❑ High repeat business
❑ Good training and support
❑ Good product/service
❑ Low competition
❑ Opportunity to learn about business
❑ An information-based model that could not be easily replicated by others

The last point was very important. Mike realized that he wasn't living in the industrial age. He was in the information age, and information is valuable. If he could provide information to people, he would be providing them with value, and he would make money in exchange for this value. People will always make a profit using valuable information.

HOW TO KEEP THE TAX AGENCY OFF YOUR BACK

Mike was starting a home business for many reasons, and being a salary earning employee, the tax benefit was one of the big reasons. He knew he could make lots of progress with his wealth when he had more capital in his hands, and a bigger tax refund was a huge source of cash. However, he also knew that the tax agents were trying to get his tax dollars. Mike wanted his business to have a reasonable expectation of profit so that a tax agent wouldn't question the validity of his business. The last thing he wanted was the *appearance* of running a sham business that had no chance of ever making money.

For this reason, he decided to use a turn-key business. A turn-key business is already built and ready to run. It is ready to go, and ready to make money. An example of a turn-key business is a franchise. Anyone who buys a franchise restaurant does not have to invent the business themselves. All they have to do is pay the price and it's theirs, ready to make money.

So Mike decided to purchase one of these turn-key businesses. But Mike couldn't afford much, let alone an expensive franchise. What he was looking for was something much more affordable, smaller, and manageable than a huge, expensive franchise. He soon learned that there are small turn-key businesses available out there, much like a micro-franchise. The purchase price of the micro-franchise Mike planned on purchasing made up part of his start-up core costs.

Mike found that buying a turn-key business was also much easier and quicker than inventing his own business, especially since he was new at business and had very little experience. A turn-key business could be purchased and be making a profit in the same day. It was far less work for Mike and was a lot faster to set up. It could be run part time too, a key factor since Mike kept his job until his profits and investments could support him. If Mike had decided that he wasn't going to buy a turn-key business, that meant he would have had to invent everything himself – something he didn't have the time, experience, or knowledge to do yet.

DESIGNED FOR PASSIVE INCOME

As he was shopping for a business, Mike started to find many turn-key businesses with a built-in passive income component. Mike's plan was to buy the business, set it up, work hard at it for a few years, then sit back and collect the income. The nature of his eventual passive income was something that had to be considered right from the start. This was critical because the last thing he wanted was to be stuck behind a counter running his business himself. He wanted to own the business and have it pay him, rather than having to pay to own a job. He started to find these businesses that were designed to create passive streams of income, which was exactly what he was looking for.

WHAT BUSINESS IS REALLY ALL ABOUT

One of the first things Mike learned about business was completely opposite to what he originally thought. He originally thought business was about accounting, factories, administration, employees, and all those details that he was learning about from books he was reading. He learned that business was really about marketing. A company could have the best operations, services, or products in the world, but if that company's marketing was ineffective, the company would be out of business very quickly. A company with better marketing and an inferior product would perform better than a company with a better product and poor marketing.

McDonald's certainly doesn't have the best hamburgers in the world, but they have the best advertising in the hamburger market. Indeed, focusing on advertising and marketing simplified things for Mike, as he didn't need to focus on the thousands of other components of business. What he needed to learn the most about business was marketing. He was looking for businesses that would teach him a lot about marketing, and provide him with production and administration as part of the turn-key solution.

WHY PEOPLE BUY FAST RED CARS

The next thing that Mike learned was that marketing was about people, their nature, and their emotions. Being an engineer, he was very logical and rational. However, Mike found that people were attracted by marketing that appealed to their emotions, not their logic.

People don't generally think, "Wow, this car is economical, practical, and safe." People are more partial to listening to the inner voice that says, "Listen to how cool that engine sounds, and that color looks so sharp, I'd love to have this car!" and "I feel so great when I drive it!" Emotions play a key role in marketing and emotions drive peoples' decision to buy. Mike had to find a business where he could practice learning how people react to their emotions and his marketing.

Business is also built upon the relationships between people. Mike began to understand that who he knew, and how they felt about doing business with him was critical to his survival in the business world.

This affected everything from his partners, employees, and joint venture partners. Simply put: If someone didn't like him, they wouldn't like doing business with him. He would rather buy the exciting red car from the salesman he liked, rather than the one he didn't like. Again, Mike noticed the feelings and emotion involved. He had to learn how to get to know people, and how to understand them and their emotions. Meeting people and building a relationship is known as networking, and it's critical to survival in the business world. It's not what Mike knew, but who he knew and how he interacted with them.

A GREAT PLACE TO START

The conclusion Mike came to was to learn more about the micro-franchises that the network marketing industry offered to see if that business model would suit his needs. At first, like most people, he really didn't know anything about the industry, but after speaking with some key business contacts and mentors, he learned that network marketing micro-franchises would provide him with everything he was looking for at this point in his life.

After spending some time learning about the industry, Mike found that network marketing is just a fancy way of saying "collecting multiple streams of referral fees by giving people valuable information from a business that is already established for me." These information-based businesses also come with the benefit of having leverage and passive income built into the business, so eventually they worked for Mike passively.

In fact, much of the network marketing industry is based on helping others learn how to build a business too. This was great because Mike knew that the best way to learn something is to teach it to someone else, so this concept had an inherent value to it. At the same time, he learned that when he bought his business, he would be have a group of trainers and teachers who would provide even more valuable resources for learning about marketing. The people he would eventually teach about business would in turn provide him with leverage as they further taught and worked with newer members of Mike's network.

After he made his decision to own a turn-key business, all that remained for Mike to do was to finalize his research and choose the companies and teams to work with. Once that was complete, he started his business and was literally in business. With the stroke of a pen, he had instant products, instant infrastructure, and instant training.

WHAT SHOULD I EXPECT?

Mike wondered what he should expect out of his new information marketing business. Once he began his part-time business in the network marketing industry, he began learning many things about business, marketing, and networking as a whole. One of his expectations was for profit, but Mike also understood that his new business wasn't a get rich quick scheme. Although a large amount of income could be built over a relatively short amount of time with his new business, it wasn't going to happen overnight. It certainly wasn't going to magically happen without any effort.

Mike was on a learning curve and knew it may take anywhere from a few months to a few years to build his knowledge and his business. He needed to remain realistic in his expectations, and know that it was going to take some time to learn about any business and ramp up revenue and profits.

From Mike's perspective, he got into business – specifically marketing pre-packaged information for a referral fee – for a number of reasons, which included:

- ☐ To own a business to invest some of his new found capital
- ☐ To generate liberated capital
- ☐ To increase his tax refund
- ☐ To learn about & practice business & marketing
- ☐ To learn about & meet business people
- ☐ To have the potential for unlimited profits
- ☐ To begin to build passive income

Mike realized that his new business had the potential to be very profitable, but that it was more of a "get wealthy gradually" program and it wasn't only about dollars and cents. His new business was a critical step in a process he was building, but it wasn't the only step. Mike explained this to everyone who was interested in his business, because he wanted them to understand the big picture and be realistic about all aspects of the business.

DIVERSIFYING PRODUCTS AND SERVICES

Once Mike had his first foundation business up and running, it started to reach a passive state and he really began to understand many aspects of business.

Then he figured he could start to focus on expanding his business and grow it into other fields.

Throughout his increasingly busy business life, he was meeting a lot of other business people with like-minded attitudes. These fellow business owners were very open to putting together deals that benefited both Mike and the other business quite well. Mike called these "win-win" situations because they benefited both parties.

These deals between two companies were called **joint ventures** in the business world, and they were quite attractive and profitable. He was able to put together several deals, including joining together with a business owner in his hometown that used Mike's business product as a promotional item, and Mike used the shop's products as a promotional item in his business.

It was a win-win situation for both of them, as they drove business to each other's companies. In addition to his own micro-franchise, joint ventures with other business owners were also providing another steady stream of passive income for him.

Mike liked the idea of using other peoples' existing business resources so much, he eventually took a course on how to become more effective at developing joint ventures between his own companies, and other companies.

TURNING SWEAT EQUITY INTO PASSIVE INCOME

Now that Mike was in business, he started to gradually turn his time and effort into passive income. It wasn't much at first, but as he put continuous full time effort into his part time business, he began to see profits as the fruits of his labour. Because Mike had chosen the business specifically to churn out passive income, his business started taking less of his time, and continued to pay him more money.

SIZING UP THE BUSINESS FOUNTAIN

Mike spent about $100 per month on core costs, plus converted $800 in personal expenses for a total of $900 per month in business expenses. This included core costs such as his supplies and advertising, and previously personal expenses, such as part of his car payment, meals and travel expenses. At Mike's tax rate, this $900 per month was $10,800 per year, and translated into a $2,700 tax refund.

Mike had access to $50,000 from his mortgage conversion, which easily funded his business and left him with about $39,000 to use elsewhere after his $10,800 in business expenses were covered. This capital overflowed from the sole proprietor business bucket into the next opportunity in the middle class wealth fountain. Mike returned to his "middle class wealth fountain" analogy:

Size of the Home Business Fountain:

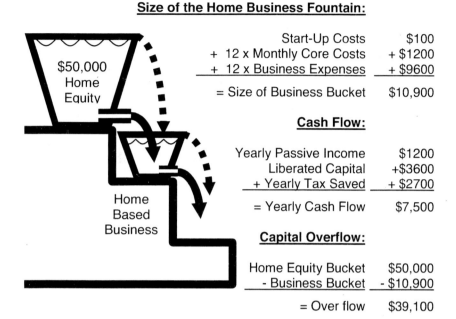

Start-Up Costs	$100
+ 12 x Monthly Core Costs	+ $1200
+ 12 x Business Expenses	+ $9600
= Size of Business Bucket	$10,900

Cash Flow:

Yearly Passive Income	$1200
Liberated Capital	+$3600
+ Yearly Tax Saved	+ $2700
= Yearly Cash Flow	$7,500

Capital Overflow:

Home Equity Bucket	$50,000
- Business Bucket	- $10,900
= Over flow	$39,100

$50,000 Home Equity

Home Based Business

It only cost Mike an extra $1200 per year to run his business, but between tax savings and profits that business generated an extra $7,500 a year in cash flow for him.

The business was only one part of the leveraged chain of events in the whole system. In the middle class wealth fountain, capital flows from one opportunity to the next. The returns from one bucket come out the spout into the next bucket, and any excess capital from one bucket overflows into the next stage. The size of each bucket is the maximum amount of capital Mike planned on placing in that opportunity. The overflow from Mike's home equity that wasn't used in his business was about $39,000, and this simply flowed into his next opportunity. This made the system self-funding, self-adjusting, and self-propagating. Mike often joked in his dry engineering sense of humour and called his flexible system "very fluid."

SUMMARY

Funding his own business as a sole proprietor with part of the capital from his converted mortgage allowed Mike to pay for his core business expenses, as well as many other business expenses he was already spending personally. This had two major financial effects: a bigger tax refund and liberated capital. He also was learning about passive income and building a business part-time as additional benefits.

Mike found it was best to first fund his own business, get the tax deductions, and then use this boosted amount of capital to invest. However, there was a maximum amount of money Mike planned on investing in his own business. Once this maximum was reached, then any overflow capital would flow into the next opportunity, including tax strategies and investments.

Now it was time for Mike to use his initial tax planning, profits, and liberated cash from his business to get the remainder of his tax back, so that eventually his investments could be fully funded with the maximum amount of capital possible. It was time for Mike to fully disarm the tax trap.

FINISHING THE INCOME TAX ESCAPE

> *"Anyone may arrange his affairs so that his taxes shall be as low as possible; he is not bound to choose that pattern which best pays the treasury. There is nothing sinister in so arranging affairs as to keep taxes as low as possible."*
>
> - Judge Learned Hand (1872-1961)
> Helvering v. Gregory Case, U. S. Court of Appeals Judge

STILL PAYING TOO MUCH TAX

Mike had been deducting much of his spending money through business expenses, and kept continually deducting the business loan interest since he started his journey, but despite these deductions he was still paying quite a bit of income tax. He was determined to reduce this tax bill even further.

Mike's expenses were divided up into three categories:

Middle Class Mike's Expenses

Mike realized that the middle class pays the most taxes out of everybody. In a marginal tax bracket system, the small amount of money that low income earners make isn't taxed very much and the rich structure their affairs to maintain their wealth. The fact that the middle class is hit the hardest, but can easily and legally avoid paying so much tax is why income taxes are another middle class trap.

Minimizing income tax is nothing new. In fact, there have been examples in court where people are encouraged to minimize the tax they pay. As Supreme Court Justice Louis Brandeis put it:

"I live in Alexandria, Virginia. Near the Supreme Court chambers is a toll bridge across the Potomac. When in a rush, I pay the dollar toll and get home early. However, I usually drive outside the downtown section of the city and cross the Potomac on a free bridge.

This bridge was placed outside the downtown Washington DC area to serve a useful social service: getting drivers to drive the extra mile to help alleviate congestion during rush hour.

If I went over the toll bridge and through the barrier without paying the toll, I would be committing tax evasion.

If, however, I drive the extra mile outside the city of Washington and take the free bridge, I am using a legitimate, logical, and suitable method of tax avoidance, and am performing a useful social service by doing so.

For my tax evasion, I should be punished. For my tax avoidance, I should be commended.

The tragedy of life today is that so few people know that the free bridge even exists."

- Louis D. Brandeis
Supreme Court Justice (1856 - 1941)

Indeed, there are ways to find and use the tax-free bridge legally and morally. In fact, many of the tax saving methods also provide a social service, much like the judge described. Mike just had to discover what these bridges looked like, and start using them.

HOW TO PAY DRASTICALLY LESS INCOME TAX

Taxes were a huge portion of Mike's expenses, so getting this money back was a substantial source of capital. But Mike could only reduce his taxes so much on his own. The two methods Mike was already using to lower his tax bill and get a bigger tax refund – loan interest and business deductions – he was doing on his own. In order to get the remainder of Mike's taxes back, he had to get outside help. All of the wealthy people he knew had help saving taxes, so why shouldn't he get help too?

Mike found a few mentors and agents to help him save tax. They all told him about a generic three-step plan that the wealthy use:

1. An individual provides a third party company a prescribed amount of money.
2. The company returns the funding gesture by facilitating certain tax benefits to the individual.
3. The individual claims the tax benefits to get tax returns that far exceed the initial outlay of capital.

At first, Mike found that many people seemed to have a problem with this concept.

"How can that be?" they would ask Mike. "How can you possibly get more back in taxes than it cost you for a strategy?"

It was all about timing and perspective. Those tax benefits may be more valuable to one person than it is to another. "Cash value" and "use value" are different amounts to different people, since one person's trash is another person's treasure. Sometimes money is traded for certain tax credits, such as when we give to charity. The charity would rather have the cash than the tax credit. Sometimes money is traded for income reduction, such as when we deduct expenses. Many of these strategies are effective, and with the right strategy the results can be magnified far past the taxpayer's initial contribution.

One weekend at a local workshop, Mike was fortunate enough to meet up with Harry, the owner of a *Harry's Hot Dogs*. Harry had already arranged for $45,000 to be invested into his own business and was in the midst of buying equipment, training his staff, and buying rights to a location. He borrowed from family, friends, banks – anyone and everyone who would lend him money. However he didn't have quite enough capital, and his budget projections was showing that his money well was going to run dry.

Even though he had raised $45,000, Harry still needed an additional $5,000 to buy supplies to get his hot dog stand going. If he didn't get the remaining $5,000 that he needed, his business would fail and he'd waste the entire $45,000 he had already raised for the business.

Mike offered to invest in Harry's company by lending him the money in return for a 50/50 partnership. Mike would be entitled to fifty percent of the profits and fifty percent of the losses as a partner. His offer of fifty percent was reasonable, as Mike could lose his entire investment of $5,000, so he needed to be compensated for this risk. Once both parties agreed to the deal, it looked like this:

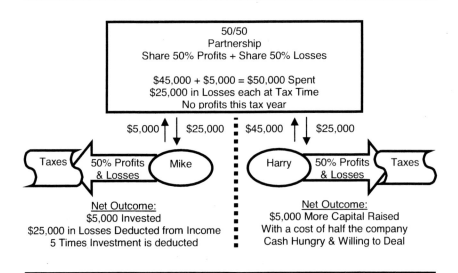

Since the deal was made before any profits happened to be made, the $50,000 total spent was called a loss and was split between the partners. Mike got $25,000 in losses, and Harry the hot dog stand owner got $25,000 in losses.

When tax time came, Mike then applied this loss against all of his personal income. Since Mike made

$60,000 that year, he got to subtract $25,000 in losses against that income, and he only was taxed on $35,000.

Mike's regular salary	**$60,000**	**Income**
Mike's half of the partnership	— **$25,000**	**Generated Loss**
Mike pays tax on this amount	**$35,000**	**Taxable Income**

Even though it only cost Mike $5,000 to do the deal, he got to deduct $25,000 – which was five times as much. Mike referred to this number five as the multiplier. This multiplier gave him the leverage for magnified returns. Depending on the circumstances and tax vehicle used, the magnified effect would be different. In this case, it was five times as much as the capital he needed to partner up.

In the end, Mike saved the taxes on $25,000, which worked out to be about $8,000 in cash for him in a tax refund.

Tax Mike paid on $60,000	**$13,000**	**Tax Paid**
Tax Mike owed on $35,000	— **$5,000**	**Tax Owed**
	$8000	**Saved Tax**

Even though it only cost Mike $5000, he got $8,000 in taxes back. Turning $5,000 into $8,000 is a 60% cash return.

Compared to the 3% return Mike averaged in mutual funds last year, 60% looked pretty attractive.

Tax Mike Saved		$8000	Savings
Partnership Costs	—	$5000	Cost
60% Cash on Cash Return		$3000	Net Gain

Mike also knew he was providing a useful social service. The hot dog stand business spent $50,000 into the economy, including sales taxes. Once the business was up and running, the employees of the business also earned a living and paid more taxes. For these reasons, tax regulators like this type of structure too. Even though Mike was saving taxes, it was paid elsewhere by other people. In addition, the tax agency had no problem with Mike investing in business deals, forming partnerships, or lending money.

This was just an example to show how the contribution can be magnified in taxes back. By no means are these exact and complete details – they just serve as an illustration for education purposes. Consulting tax professionals before implementing structures like this is always a good idea.

The best part about this for Mike was that with one simple contribution he could potentially eliminate a large amount of taxes. There was no more worrying about smaller deductions and minor credits here and there. In one fell swoop he saved the rest of his taxes that he couldn't reduce through his own interest or expense deductions.

THE NEW PROBLEM

Since Mike had discovered numerous sources of capital – home equity, business expense tax refunds, business loan tax refunds, profits, and liberated capital – finding the money to enter into business deals like this was no longer an issue. Now the issue became finding business situations such as Harry's that needed his capital. Mike didn't exactly know many desperate hot dog stand owners willing to give up half of his company. Mike needed help with the search.

Lucky for Mike, he didn't have to find these opportunities himself. He found out from his mentors that there are numerous companies that create tax saving programs anywhere from venture capital, to initial public offerings, to medicine charities, to private jet planes, to computer software donations that he could use to get more tax back. It was just a matter of research and due diligence to find the best firm for him. Mike chose to hire a boutique accounting firm to do the searching, structuring, and legal legwork for him for various deals that gave him a magnified tax benefit. All Mike had to do was provide the funding, and wait for tax time to arrive.

For Mike, it was a classic win-win scenario. If the businesses failed, he got to claim a leveraged amount of losses on his taxes. If the businesses prospered, then he got a leveraged amount of profits in his pocket. He positioned himself to gain either way.

SIZING THE TAX BUCKET

Just as Mike had sized the home equity and business buckets of the middle class wealth fountain, Mike also sized up the tax bucket. There was a maximum amount of money Mike planned on putting into a third party tax strategy to help reduce his taxes. Once this maximum allotment was reached, any excess capital overflowed into the other liberated capital opportunities such as converting bad debt and investing.

The tax stage of the middle class wealth fountain was limited by the amount of income tax Mike owed. After all, he could only get back as much tax as he originally owed. Mike also had to plan to take into account the hired firm's projections for how much in tax benefits he may be entitled to when the year ended. Mike was able to reduce his original $60,000 salary down to $50,000 with his other deductions, such as his home business. However, his target income to pay tax on was $25,000.

This created a wide open "income window" that Mike wanted to close. Mike estimated that he would get 5 times as many expenses as it cost him to use the strategy, just like his deal with Harry, so he divided his income window by 5. The result is how much he put into his hired firm's tax strategy. His tax bucket size became ($50k - $25k) / 5 = $5,000.

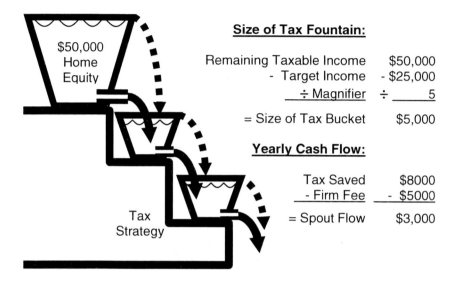

Size of Tax Fountain:		
Remaining Taxable Income	$50,000
- Target Income	- $25,000
÷ Magnifier	÷ 5
= Size of Tax Bucket	$5,000

Yearly Cash Flow:

Tax Saved	$8000
- Firm Fee	- $5000
= Spout Flow	$3,000

Any capital that wasn't used in the tax bucket, as well as the tax return created by the strategy, flows to the next bucket in the fountain. This means the cash flow that was produced by the business, plus the home equity overflow that wasn't used by the business, plus the tax refund flows through the tax strategy and into the investments.

WHAT'S IN A NAME?

Why was this called tax reduction or tax compression, and not tax elimination? Recall that it took $5,000 in order for Mike to reduce his taxable income by $25,000 from losses in Harry's business. This means it cost Mike about 20% to use this strategy.

$5,000 Cost / $25,000 Return = 20% Effective Tax Rate

Since he started with a 25% tax rate, he is effectively reducing – or compressing – his tax rate down to 20%. If Mike was only in a 15% tax bracket, this strategy would not be any good to him, as the cost for the strategy would be higher than the benefits. In this case, he would have to search for a lower cost option, for example one that gave him $7 in deductions for every $1 in the program. This would give him a reduced rate of 14% ($1/$7). He would be reducing his tax rate by 1% in this case from 15% down to 14%. Not very much, but every little bit counts.

This rate reduction concept can also be applied to the reduced tax rate that a home based business gets the owner. If it costs $100 in core costs (inventory and advertising) but $1500 in expenses are deducted from taxes, then the compressed rate is $100 divided by $1500, or 6%. The home-based business compression calculation allowed Mike to pre-determine how much his core costs were, and how many expenses he was going to write off, thereby designing the reduced rate. Someone in a lower tax bracket might have to use more home business deductions and less third party strategies, whereas someone in a higher tax bracket would use a different combination of both. Being able to massage the numbers offered Mike and the people he was helping great flexibility.

ALL EXPENSES PAID

Mike was reducing his income tax liability down to practically zero. However, there was a basic cost for Mike to save taxes and make this money. This was the cost of interest, the core cost of the home-based business and the cost to fund the third-party tax strategy. But, the money Mike saved in taxes more than paid for these expenses, so overall he was always ahead.

Remember that "liberated capital" Mike had because he paid for his expenses with a business loan? This non-borrowed liberated capital funded his third party tax strategy. He also used tax refunds from previous years to fund it. Any remaining capital needed came from underperforming investments, or lastly a loan.

Mike had developed a three-step process to save tax:

1. Deduct his business and investment loan interest.
2. Deduct his sole proprietorship business expenses.
3. Deduct his third party expenses.

Now that Mike had successfully accessed capital through his mortgage and substantially reduced his taxes, Mike set his sites on the next step: finding the best place to invest his money.

INVESTMENT UNLEARNING

"Wall Street is the only place where people ride to in a Rolls Royce to get advice from those who take the subway."

- Warren Buffet
Billionaire American Investor

MIDDLE CLASS INVESTMENT MARKETING

Finally, it was time for Mike to put his capital into an investment that would grow his money. He noticed that much of the investment marketing was geared towards the middle class market. And it seemed the outcome was keeping the middle class firmly entrenched in the middle class.

Most of the advice offered by mainstream financial marketing literature was to simply hand money over to them so they could get guaranteed returns while Mike was asked to wear all of the risk. Essentially, their tactics could be summed up as "buy and hope" or "park and pray" – risky moves that were made without any real knowledge, risk management, due diligence, or sound investing strategy. Mike didn't want high-risk investments. He wanted low-risk investments with high returns.

Spotting and escaping the middle class investment traps was not about ignorance – there were plenty of well educated investors out there who weren't making much money – it was about unlearning unsupportive investment beliefs. Mike found the often paraphrased Josh Billings to be especially apt. Billings said: "It's not what we don't know that is the problem, but what we do know that just isn't correct."

In talking directly to wealthy investors, Mike discovered three of his previous accepted central pillars of investing didn't stand up to scrutiny. First, he found that the return on investments he had been trained to accept, didn't need to be accepted at all. Secondly, the old adage that investing is risky didn't need to be true if the right steps were followed. And finally, that the motives of the investment industry wasn't always focused on his best interests.

WHY EXPECT SUCH LOW RETURNS?

Mike had always been told eight percent returns are good returns. However, as he spoke with his wealthy friends, he found that they would never consider investments returning a mere eight percent – especially not when it was entirely plausible that many of those investments had lost 20 percent or more in a single year in the past. His wealthy friends said they expected a minimum of twenty percent returns on their money and most demanded far more.

When Mike reported this to his middle class friends, they were truly worried that he was being scammed. But Mike had already seen it was possible to get 125 percent returns from a home-based business and 60 percent returns from effective tax strategies. He was open to the idea that maybe there really were better ways of generating high returns outside of what he had been conditioned to hear about in the mainstream media.

Mike found that one of the biggest causes of the belief that low returns are the only option available is overregulation. It seemed like every time something went wrong with a major investment, Mike read in the paper about another layer of regulation, rules, or security that was added. Every time there was a layer of bureaucracy or regulation, money gets taken out of the pockets of investors. The investment industry certainly wasn't paying for it. The increasingly disproportionate number of accountants, lawyers, and regulators who write and process the paperwork and conduct audits cost money and all that eats into investors' profits. Executives become more focused on the reporting requirements for the newspapers than actually making profits. Instead of fostering business, this simply stifles it and lowers returns even further. Mike heard one businessman state during a speech that regulation took up over one third of his company's resources, just to deal with the paperwork.

How much could these extra layers of middlemen possibly cost investors? In 2006, the New York Times reported that Goldman Sachs alone paid out over more than $16 billion in bonuses to their investment house staff. That's more money than the 2006 Gross Domestic Product of the entire country of Cyprus and it went straight to brokers. That could have been used to foster business, educate investors, or reward investors with higher returns. Instead, since it costs so much to pay for bureaucracy, regulation, and middlemen, businesses and investors get dinged with the bill in the form of lower profits and returns. Mike found that there were other sources of drainage too, such as highly overpaid executives of public companies with money that could have gone back to shareholders – the people taking all the risks.

Also, in an effort to protect investors from risk, the same regulators keep investors from opportunity. In the international investment arena, the Standard and

Poor's Guide on International Investment Funds[10] reported returns of 30% to 385% for the international funds. But these funds aren't available to those investors of certain countries or to investors who don't have high income and or a high net worth (referred to as accredited investors). Non-accredited investors with lower incomes and low net worth get the so-called benefit of being protected from these types of vehicles. Mike certainly did not appreciate this unwanted and unwelcome protection from higher returns.

Mike began to realize that because of this protection the average investor doesn't even realize these higher returns exist, let alone have the ability to participate in them. Similarly, many of the private company offerings aren't available to smaller investors due to the same income and/or net worth limitations. Thankfully though, Mike did find some notable exceptions.

One of Mike's early investments was in a close friend's e-commerce start-up company. Mike was only legally able to participate in this investment because the owner was a close friend of his and Mike got a regulatory exemption because of this friendship. Even though the investment ended up producing a handsome quadruple digit return (more than 1000%) when the company was sold, Mike would not have been eligible for the investment if he had not been a close friend of the

---

[10] Standard & Poor's Guide to Offshore Investment Funds, ISBN 978-0952855828

founder. Other non-friend and family investors essentially already had to be millionaires.

These barriers to investing contribute to people not believing such high returns are possible. Contrast the low return belief of the middle class with the fact that many of the sophisticated investors won't examine any opportunity below a 20% annual return. Many of the banks and venture capitalists demand a minimum of 25% to 40% yearly return or higher, which is well documented on government and industry websites.

Mike had to re-condition his mind to accept that high returns are possible with relatively low risk. Once he did, a whole other world of investments opened up. This was the world of investments that his wealthy mentors had been participating in for years. Mike knew that if he didn't believe he could earn more than eight percent, he would never earn more than eight percent. This trap wasn't simply about getting low returns – the trap was also not knowing that they are low returns in the first place.

HOW MUCH ARE YOU AT RISK?

"The biggest risk is not taking one at all," is common investment mantra. However this doesn't mean good investors make risky moves. Rather those good investors find good deals and then act. Before Mike could act, he realized he had to understand the real risks of his investments. Once he knew the real risks, he could manage the risk more effectively.

What Mike found was that the same nasty over regulation that lowers returns and expectations of returns doesn't add security to the investment. There are investments that still fail everyday despite all the regulation. Risk cannot be eliminated from investing, it can only be reduced, and bureaucracy isn't the way to reduce it – due diligence is.

Investors have the same risk of losing their money with or without the bureaucracy. Mike thought about it this way: If executives of the corrupt public company Enron Inc. had more paperwork to fill out, would the shareholders have been any safer? If anything, this bureaucracy should be educating investors about risk, returns, costs, and due diligence. This is the only way to become educated about the investment and manage the risk, instead of masking it with regulation and pretending the investment world is now safer.

A simple rule to judge what the risk can be is to determine the probability and impact of loss. Probability means what are the odds that the investment will not provide the return I expect? This part of risk can be reduced by performing good due diligence as Mike discovered later. Due diligence means finding out the essential information to reduce the odds of the investment going sour.

Simple Risk Analysis

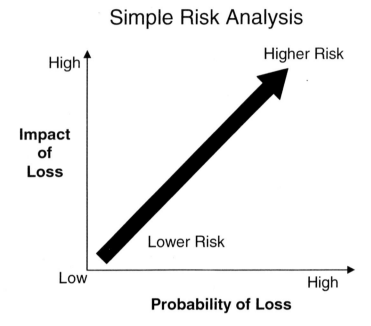

Impact means what happens if the possibility becomes a certainty? The impact risk can be reduced by managing the terms of the investment, such as collateral that is held for security, transparency of the business, or repayment terms, which Mike discovered or stipulated while conducting due diligence.

The trick, Mike discovered, was determining the possibility and impact of loss for each investment decision made, and then finding ways to reduce both of these factors. This avoids the trap of making risky decisions. This risk analysis applies to every investment, from the simplest term deposit, to stocks and bonds, to private placements of capital.

Another simple way to measure risk is upside versus downside. How much did Mike stand to lose, compared to how did he stand to gain? Mike quickly determined if he stood to gain a potential return of 8%, but the potential loss is more than 20%, it wasn't a reasonable cost/benefit. However if he stood to lose 4% but he could make 20% the investment was substantially better.

Risk is also not related to return. This is quickly proven with an example. If one bank offers Mike an interest rate of 1.5% on its deposits, but another bank offers 3%, is the 3% bank investment twice as risky as the first? No, they are almost the same investment with the same risk even though the return of one investment is double the other investment.

> Mike found that risk is not related to return.

Is an investment in rental real estate that gives 20% returns twice as risky as a 10% return in the stock market? Not necessarily. If the real estate deal goes bad, the investor simply seizes the property and gets the original capital back. However, if the stock market doesn't perform the 10% return as expected, there is nothing the investor can do. The real estate return that is twice as big has far less risk. Once this disconnect between risk and rate of return is understood to be separate, investors can become more comfortable believing that there are safe high return investments out there. The wealthy don't take large risks. They take large, safe profits.

WHO GIVES YOU ADVICE?

Another lesson Mike learned from his wealthy mentors was that wealthy individuals don't pay for empty advice – they pay for performance. If the advice didn't perform, they took their money elsewhere. Compare that to the typical middle class mutual fund. The wealthy may use funds like these, but how the manager is paid is often structured differently. For example, many of the managed futures funds in the marketplace are paid on a performance basis. They may take 25% of the profits they gain their clients, but if no gains are made, the managers don't get paid. That's a **vested interest** which creates an incentive for the manager to make their client money. This differs greatly from the fees that are taken right off the top in much of the conventional mutual fund industry. Mike took a close look at how his advisors, agents, and managers were being paid for their services – did it come from the deal transaction itself, or from a percentage of the money they made for him? Did they have their own money in the investment they were recommending to him? It was even better if the manager or agent was living off the investments that were being recommended to him, and not the sales commission only.

> Managed Futures are similar to hedge funds, only they use futures contracts exclusively, not stocks or bonds.

If someone who makes a recommendation only gets paid if the client makes money, they have a vested interest in making their client money. If the client doesn't make money, they don't make money. Middle Class Mike would have never even known of this service if not for his wealthy friends.

Much of the advice that was given to Mike's middle class friends and family was from a salesperson who had a commission to earn from the sale itself, instead of earning the money based on the gains of the client. If the advice was bad, well, that was the client's problem as the salesperson had already been paid. This is not how the wealthy invest their money.

Mike started to think like Warren Buffet. "Does my advisor take the subway or drive a Rolls-Royce? Did he pay for the Rolls from the investments that he is advising me to make and from profit sharing he has arranged with me?"

These were the types of investment advisors and mangers that Mike was searching for. Whenever someone offered Mike advice, he would usually start off by saying "You can have 20% of whatever profit you make for me." Contrast this to those who make money even though the recommended investments loses money. Should someone get paid even though his or her advice was bad? Should we take advice from those who don't take their own advice? If the advice is good, are they wealthy because of that advice?

Mike found that another part of the investment trap is listening to the government or industry-funded agencies when they hand out investment advice. Mike realized that these agencies often have ulterior motives in mind, such as how to gather more taxes, earn more fees, pay fewer benefits, or control the investment arena more tightly.

Mike began to question why any agency was recommending a certain investment vehicle or structure. He wanted to hear that the more money the client makes the more money the adviser makes. Sometimes it appeared that way only on the surface.

Canadian RRSP note #1: The RRSP limit is only several thousands of dollars. If a wealthy woman makes $1 Million per year, is a RRSP useful to her?

Canadian RRSP note #2: Canada Revenue Agency advertises for you to invest in a RRSP. The bigger your RSP is, the fewer benefits the Canadian government will pay you. Is the RRSP in your best interest, or the government's?

Canadian RRSP note #3: Capital gains get better tax treatment outside an RRSP than inside. Where is the best place to earn capital gains?

The answer to escaping the middle class investment trap began with expecting higher returns, demanding less bureaucracy, cutting out unnecessary middlemen, seeing through mass marketing of bad vehicles, paying for performance, knowing and managing the risks, and getting directly to the investment. By doing this, Mike found higher returns, more transparency, and less risk. In order to become wealthy, Middle Class Mike needed to think like the wealthy, and invest like the wealthy. For some of these opportunities, this required Mike to get to accredited investor[11] status as soon as possible to open them up. It definitely required Mike to hang around the right people, especially those who were already using these types of vehicles. Mike knew he would earn within 10% of the income of the people he hung around. It was time to start hanging around people who were successful in their investments.

Investing like the wealthy started with unlearning his old underperforming investment knowledge. Once he had shed this shackle of bad information, Mike could learn to invest like a millionaire.

---

[11] It varies between jurisdictions, but an accredited (or sometimes called "sophisticated") investor is generally defined as someone with over $1 Million in net worth, or who earns at least two hundred thousand dollars per year.

INVESTING LIKE A MILLIONAIRE

"How many millionaires do you know who have become wealthy by investing in savings accounts? I rest my case."

Robert G. Allen

Author, *Multiple Streams of Income*

Once Mike had this system of unlocking his hidden capital and knew what *not* to look for in an investment, it was time to put it to good use sending him income on a regular basis.

There were specific criteria that Mike was searching for in his investments. He built this list of criteria after months of researching how wealthy people invest their hard earned money.

Ideally, Mike was looking for:

❑ Security and Collateral
❑ Cash Flow Payments
❑ Tax Efficiency
❑ Steady High Rates of Return
❑ Asset Protection
❑ Estate Progression
❑ Investment History
❑ Good Due Diligence Results

SECURITY

First on the priority list was security. Mike went to a lot of effort to raise his capital, he didn't want to lose it if his investments went south. What Mike looked for was investments with collateral for the money he was going to pour into the business. This way, if the opportunity went bad he could seize the assets of the company and liquidate them to get some or all of his capital back. Just like a bank wouldn't provide a loan to Mike if he didn't have collateral, he wouldn't provide his investment dollars if he didn't have something to hold in return to protect his principle.

Mike compared this criterion to the standard mutual fund model used by the middle class. Mutual funds are mainly comprised of common stock therefore they have no security and no collateral behind them. The stock itself is based on a market driven price point, and can drop in an instant at the whim of the masses. The returns are doomed to the same fate. That's not very secure. Generally, there is little or no security at all behind the stock market investments. If the stock didn't perform, or the price dropped dramatically, it is too bad for the investor, there is no recourse the investor can take, and that is where the story ends.

Mike found it didn't have to be this way. He could have security, protection, and high rates in the same investment vehicle. Real estate was a good example of a secure collateralized investment, because if the investment went bad Mike could seize the land and building to sell it off to get part of the investment back. However, he had to be careful as market forces also determine real estate prices, so real estate is not completely infallible. Thus he kept only a portion of his portfolio exposed to real estate. Mike made sure that if real estate was part of the deal, he or his company was put on the title of the deed so that it couldn't be sold without him knowing about it.

Mike also found general security agreements could cover an array of assets backing the investment. Periodic audits of what the company held as assets were reported back to the investors reassuring them that the assets haven't been reduced as part of their collateral. Alternatively, Mike found buying into a partnership actually allowed him to own a portion of the business and its profits and losses directly.

All of this protection comes from the investment being made in something tangible that can be re-sold. When the capital is used for something intangible, such as a service, the risk is higher. A service cannot be liquidated if the investment goes bad.

When Mike looked at the collateral securing the investment, he looked to the equity to debt ratio to determine his margin of safety. This was how much the company's assets were worth divided by the amount they owed to creditors. For example, a company with ten dollars of assets for every one dollar that they owe investors has a very attractive 10:1 ratio. The company's balance sheet shows the worth of the company, and how much hard asset security they could offer as security in return for a cash investment. An independent auditor could verify the validity of the balance sheet. Mike hired lawyers and accountants together with his group of fellow investors to perform this function to help him evaluate his opportunities.

Some of the time the assets that were backing Mike's investment were not liquid. In other words, they were not easy to sell, as they were invested in buildings, land, or equipment. The company wasn't going to sell these assets to raise cash, that's why they have brought in investors with cash. However, even though these assets can't be used to pay for employees, they can be used as an excellent source to secure investment capital.

Alternatively, there are certain over the counter vehicles on the market that offer no risk to the investment principle, such as principle protected notes, segregated funds, or leveraged bank investments where the money never leaves the bank account. Mike also added these to his list of options available, but kept in mind that the returns may be too low to accept.

Whatever the method, steps can be taken to help protect an investment against loss. The banks protect their investment, the wealthy do too, and Mike was able to do it now also.

CASH FLOW

Second, Mike looked for solid periodic cash flow in his investment options. Much like how he analyzed his house and his business in terms of cash flow, he needed to analyze his other investments in terms of cash flow too. Remember that

> **Cash flow** was how much money was coming into Mike's bank account every month from the investment.

Mike didn't consider his house a good investment, mainly because a paid-off house didn't pay his bills because it produced zero cash flow. Actually, it was negative cash flow as it took money out of his pocket every month to live in the house.

What Mike was looking for was the details of when he would have access to his return on investment (ROI). Monthly access was excellent, quarterly access was good, and yearly access was ok. Anything longer than one year he didn't really like because he needed to

pay his bills with this money once he quit his job or
retired.

Mike even considered price appreciation of the
investment as a type of long term cash flow as he knew
at some point he would want to take his money out of
the investment. After all, as an investor Mike knew that
is what an investment is for. In pure appreciation plays
– buy low, sell high – selling off the investment is known
as an "exit strategy" and Mike needed to know what his
exit strategy would be long before he made the
investment.

TAX EFFICIENCY

Mike went to a lot of effort to minimize his taxes,
so he wanted to choose his investments to stay
optimized for tax efficiency. Each time he looked at an
investment, he took a look at when and how much tax
he would have to pay on the return. A good investment
would have him paying very little tax a long time from
now. A not so good investment would mean paying a
lot of tax very soon. Ideally, Mike wanted to be able to
control when and how much tax he paid. With the help
of his mentors, lawyers, and a network of other investors
who were doing well with their money, he did find that
investments exist that can owe very little in the way of
taxes.

For example, investments in companies that flow
through revenue and expenses help offset the taxable

profit, such as limited partnerships or types of flow-through shares. Certain distributions from a trust, tax shelters, dividends, and capital gains all get preferential tax treatment in Canada. Mike looked for these types of characteristics in his investment search, and when he found them they added to the value that the investment offered.

STEADY HIGH RATES OF RETURN

Investing was about making money. Mike knew he didn't need to tolerate poor rates of return and that indeed, he should demand consistent annual returns of at least 18%. After all, if he shot for the stars he might at least hit the moon.

What is the benefit of a consistent positive rate of return? Mike took a look at the past 80 years of stock market returns. Some years were positive returns in the 20% to 30% range, some years were negative returns, dropping as much as 20% or more.

If Mike had invested $100 in 1928, the variable stock portfolio would have been worth **$146,062** in 2005. When Mike took the average of the up and down returns, the average was 11.72 %. He then compared these variable stock market returns to a consistently positive rate of return. If Mike had invested the same $100 over the same period of time at a fixed rate of

The table of these fixed rate calculations comparisons are listed in Annex A of this book.

.11.72% he would have **$566,350**, over three times as much. Mike proved to himself that a consistently positive rate of return was much more profitable than a variable rate of return that had negative years. For this reason, Mike ideally searched for fixed rates of return, such as promissory notes and contracts. Realizing the world is not ideal, Mike also accepted a consistent "best effort" return, such as when he collected rent from real estate. It wasn't fixed or guaranteed, but it was consistently high. Much of the time the type of payment (fixed or best effort) was a trade-off for another benefit such as tax benefits, liquidity or security.

There were other benefits of having a fixed rate of return instead of variable rates. Since Mike planned to use this money in order to live, he needed to know that it was going to be there when he needed it. The last thing he wanted to happen was to have a 10% or 20% drop in his assets or income that was needed to put food on his table.

Since he knew what his minimum rate of return was going to be he could plan accordingly and sleep easy knowing how much money he had to spend. A fixed rate of return completely removed market risk from his portfolio. The probability of him not knowing what his return was going to be was reduced to almost zero.

Mike discovered a number of investment options through his network of friends and business associates that allowed him to have consistently high returns on his money.

The first investment he made was in a private gold mining company. Mike thought this was an excellent move in terms of security because gold was excellent collateral as a universal store for value around the world. Gold also happened to be a very profitable business once they got the funding, so Mike was able to secure a 27% fixed rate of return on his capital. If the business didn't pay him as agreed, he could take the land that had proven gold deposits in it and sell it to any other mining company. Also the company agreed to flow through expenses to reduce Mike's tax liability on the capital gains profit he made, so it was a double feature.

Next Mike invested in a private real estate investment company that took his capital and purchased large commercial buildings and leased them out. Taking the tax benefits into account, Mike made the equivalent of more than 20% annually on his capital, and it was backed by the real estate.

The next move was into an insured promissory note from a business consortium group. Not only was the note secured by the assets of the company, the company also placed an insurance policy on the borrowed principle, as well as the 18% return they promised to their lenders. Although this 18% return was a slightly lower return than what Mike was now used to, he decided to accept it due to the increased level of security that the insurance policy provided. In this case, his fixed rate of return had a dual source of collateral for security, instead of just one main source.

Mike then came across a variety of products where Mike's capital never left his bank account. One vehicle offered profit sharing on various real estate or global financing projects just by using Mike's credit to help build their business. Another opportunity that appeared was where traders had access to the bank's fractional reserve abilities to use Mike's deposits without ever having to remove them. Although these vehicles were very sophisticated behind the scenes, from Mike's perspective since his money never left his bank account it offered incredible security with very little risk.

Accessing these opportunities was made easier for Mike by knowing the right people or by being an accredited investor to have the doors opened. The sooner an investor becomes accredited, the sooner many more high return investments will become available. However, there are other creative investments in the marketplace in which non-accredited investors can participate. The key was for Mike to search out investments with fixed or consistent high rates of return for his portfolio, no matter what his current net worth was.

Mike's mentors and investment contacts became an enormous asset when it came to finding these high rate of return opportunities.

The way Mike remembered how to treat his investment portfolio was to think about how a bank treats their investments. The bank always asks for security for the loan, so did Mike. The bank asks for the borrower to pay them regularly, so did Mike. The bank always knew they were going to make a positive consistent amount of money – so did Mike.

ASSET PROTECTION & ESTATE PROGRESSION

Another aspect Mike was concerned with had more to do with structure than the investment itself: asset protection and estate progression. After escaping the middle class traps, the last thing Mike wanted to have happen was to have his estate taken or reduced in value by someone else, such as a creditor or the government. It was important to him to have his income producing assets sheltered away and protected from harm.

Mike recalled the story Rockefeller told of "Owning nothing – but controlling everything." Mike set up his investments this way, so that he controlled them but didn't always directly own them. He noticed this structure was similar to when someone owns a corporation. Mike may not own the company car since the corporation owns it – but he was the only one with the keys to drive it. Mike controlled how the company's investments were spent, but because he didn't own them he couldn't be sued personally for it or lose it in a divorce.

Another way Mike maintained protection was with trusts and by using an international jurisdiction with strong estate laws and no or low taxes.

Everybody Mike knew was different, and good mentors, advisors, and professionals were able to help tell how an individual would best benefit. However, the bottom line was the same across the board: by controlling the asset instead of owning it, Mike could get all the benefits, and none of the downside. He would be able to protect his assets from harm while using them, and pass them on to his children seamlessly when he died.

HISTORY

Another aspect Mike wanted to see in an investment was past success and third party references who could verify claims. The less history there was behind an opportunity, the higher the risk of failure or default. Typically, if Mike was going to investigate an opportunity that had not been around for a few years, he needed to know the people running the program or the company quite well. Only by knowing the company principles and conducting thorough due diligence would he consider investing in an opportunity that didn't have a solid history backing it up - and even then it would be on a risk adjusted basis. This means that Mike would put enough of his capital in the investment to have a positive effect his portfolio, but would keep the amount of capital small enough so that if the deal didn't perform it wouldn't ruin his net worth. This is where the risk analysis of the investment became quite useful.

DUE DILIGENCE

Due diligence was another activity Mike performed to learn about the investment and decrease his risk exposure. Due diligence is the basic investigation into the details of a potential investment. As Mike read in her book *Wealth Cycle Investing*, Loral Langemeier described five components of conducting proper due diligence:

❑ **Data** – Get the numbers and terms associated with the deal. The first place to start is to see if the investor can get in on the deal with the minimum investment required, and if the rate of return is high enough to make it worthwhile. Mike did not accept anything lower than double digit returns, and he preferred capital participation minimums to be no more than 20% of his total net worth.

❑ **Discussion** – Ask mentors, advisors, business partners, and other investors what they think of the deal. Leveraging their experience and knowledge helped Mike make a list of questions and get a feel for the opportunity.

❑ **Discovery** – Explore the opportunity in depth. Visit the offices, work sites, and employees to ask them the tough questions derived in the first two steps.

❑ **Diagnosis** – Analyse all the information gathered and run it by the team again for further comments and analysis.

❑ **Decision** – Yes or No. Mike avoided being caught up in "analysis paralysis" or a state on constantly "kicking the tires." Once all the information was gathered and analysed, Mike either took action or moved on.

Mike knew that all his investment criteria was an ideal list, and that no one investment may have every single component he was looking for. There is no one perfect investment. When he made decisions, he really had to compare the relative pros and cons of his options on the table. He may give up a long history for more security. He may trade-off less security for high liquidity and a high rate of return. Weighing the pros and cons of real life opportunities helped him make initial decisions whether to get into an investment or not, as well as whether to stay in a current investment or liquidate it in favour of another.

Taking all of these steps got Mike farther away from the middle class way of investing methods (buy and hope) and closer to the Millionaire way of investing (buy a direct piece of the profits). Instead of being lazy about the investment choices he made, he analyzed it against all of his criteria before making a choice.

TEAMWORK

Mike really saw a huge positive difference in his wealth building when he hung around and listened to the right types of people. These were people who were looking for business and investment opportunities too, and often just shared these connections with Mike. Once Mike started seeking out and listening to wealthy friends, mentors, business partners and professionals, his investment options opened up. The right types of people helped Mike connect with opportunities and helped him with his due diligence. After all, ten heads were better than one. An amazing thing happened when Mike started looking for people and opportunities to connect with – the people and opportunities suddenly appeared and became very obvious to him. Sometimes it was all about knowing what he wanted, and keeping his eyes open to see it.

Mike saw that all of these components to investing were used by the wealthy to help put their capital to work so they didn't have to. Investing at this high impact level may seem like more work than the traditional lazy way, but when the right parts and people are in place it can be quite quick and easy. Besides, doing the upfront legwork to opening these doors was worth it. Mike would rather have worked hard and become rich than have been lazy and stayed broke.

More and more relatively safe, yet high rate of return vehicles started coming across Mike's desk and he went through each one determining which he would invest in, and which he would pass on. Eventually, all of his market risk was eliminated as he sold his stock and mutual fund portfolio, and it was replaced with an average rate of return of 25%. Now he had truly replicated exactly what his wealthy mentors had been doing for years. Investing wisely was the final step in escaping the middle class.

PUTTING IT ALL TOGETHER

The value of the whole is greater than the sum of the individual parts. The increase in the value of assets as a result of their combination.

- Definition of "Synergy"

Mike's story was looking like a very happy ending indeed. Mike escaped the mortgage trap by leveraging his home to access capital, pay less tax, and then used that same home as the base for a home-based business. He slipped out of the tax trap by reducing his income tax bill to zero. He evaded the investment trap by unlearning his bad middle-class habits and replacing them with a knowledge that he could invest in secure, high return products. All of this combined to build Mike a steady stream of passive income that launched him into financial freedom. The real goal of owning his own life and not being hostage to an employer was a becoming a reality.

Much like a symphony orchestra is much more powerful than any one instrument, each component played into the next to vault Mike forward to a life of financial freedom in less than his ten year target.

Here's a summary of Mike's highlights and benefits:

1. Mortgage Principle Payment & Re-borrow: Unlocked capital, increased and prolonged his tax refunds, allowed him to seize higher return opportunities;

2. Home Business: Created profits, passive income, experience, allowed him to deduct the business loan interest, and convert many of his non-deductible personal expenses into deductible business expenses;

3. Third Party Tax Reduction Strategy: Recovered the rest of his taxes, lowered his tax rate as much as possible, boosted his available capital;

4. Safe High Return Investments: A safe place to wisely invest the created capital, which created more passive income to live free!

Each component of the system feeds into the next portion. The capital from the house feeds the business and investments. The tax benefits and income from the business feed into the third party tax program. The tax refunds further fuel the investments. The entire system works in complete synergy.

It was important to be aware of the size of the buckets in the wealth fountain when Mike used his capital. For instance, there was a limit to how much Mike needed to put into his home business and tax strategies. Eventually there came a point in time where he had more capital than he could put into his business or tax strategy. At this point, he placed this overflow of capital into the next step, the tax strategy, until that was filled too. Then the excess capital would flow directly into his investments or convert bad debt into good debt. Mike once again returned to the wealth fountain analogy to paint a visual image of what was going on with his system. The wealth fountain was now complete.

The Complete Middle Class Wealth Fountain

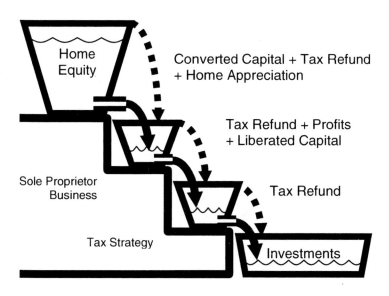

155

Mike's capital flowed to where it was best used until that segment of the fountain was full. Then it flowed to the next best opportunity. Once the structure was in place, Mike was able to make a number of investments and use those to live off the passive income. In the end, Mike simply approached his trough full of investments at the bottom of the wealth fountain, and filled his cup up to drink.

BALANCING THE BOOKS

When Mike began his wealth journey, he was just starting out with his house and was in the process of converting his mortgage into an investment loan.

Year Before Mike Escaped the Traps

Step	Bank Account	Total Debt
Mortgage Outstanding		$225,000
After Tax Wages / Salary	$34,200	
Regular Mortgage Interest Payment	-$14,400	
Regular Mortgage Principle Payment	-$4,800	-$4,800
Pay Personal Bills	-$15,000	
Balance	$0	$220,200

Mike reduced his debt to $220,200 with nothing in the bank account. Mike was paying the maximum amount of taxes, and had no capital for investments at all.

Using the same salary and wages, the same mortgage, and the same bills – but a different structure and strategy – Mike could boost his accounts one year after another by implementing his trap-free system.

After Applying the Escape System

Step	Bank Account	Total Debt
Mortgage Outstanding		$225,000
After Tax Wages / Salary	$34,200	
Regular Mortgage Interest Payment	-$14,400	
Regular Mortgage Principle Payment	-$4,800	-$4,800
Pre-Pay Mortgage	-$6,000	-$6,000
Pay Personal Bills	-$5,400	
Pay Expenses with Business Loan		$10,800
Third Party Tax Strategy	-$3,000	
Invest Remaining Cash	-$600	
Tax Refund	$6,900	
Investments Mature	$708	
Business Profits	$1,200	
Repay extra loan	-$4,800	-$4,800
Balance	**$4,008**	$220,200

Mike's ending amount of debt is exactly the same as before, but he has more than $4,000 more in his bank account. Because Mike made some strategic re-arrangements of his finances, his bank account has much more money in it.

When Mike wasn't organizing his financial affairs this way, he was losing this amount of money in his bank account every year.

To make an even comparison of "before" and "after" scenarios, the "after" table shows that Mike paid off the extra business/investment loan. In reality, Mike didn't pay off the loan or cash in the investments. That was just shown here for comparison purposes. What he did was leave everything invested so that it compounded year after year. This compounding and saving enabled Mike to replace his salary and become financially free within seven years. Before the decade ended he controlled over a million dollars in income producing assets.

	House Value	HELOC Investment	Tax Saved	Business Generated	Total Investment Value
Start	$250,000	$50,000	$0	$0	$50,000
1	$265,000	$82,689	$6,900	$1,200	$90,789
2	$280,900	$120,483	$16,921	$3,916	$141,320
3	$297,754	$164,028	$29,792	$7,121	$200,941
4	$315,619	$214,046	$46,215	$10,903	$271,163
5	$334,556	$271,343	$67,046	$15,365	$353,754
6	$354,630	$336,819	$93,337	$20,631	$450,787
7	$375,908	$411,480	$126,369	$26,844	$564,694
8	$398,462	$496,447	$167,705	$34,176	$698,328
9	$422,370	$592,970	$219,247	$42,828	$855,046
10	$447,712	$702,446	$271,210	$48,158	**$1,038,795**

HOW THINGS CHANGE OVER TIME

Year over year, his house went up with inflation and his mortgage went down as he paid it off. This meant Mike was able to borrow and invest even more HELOC. This built the HELOC investment portion of Mike's portfolio.

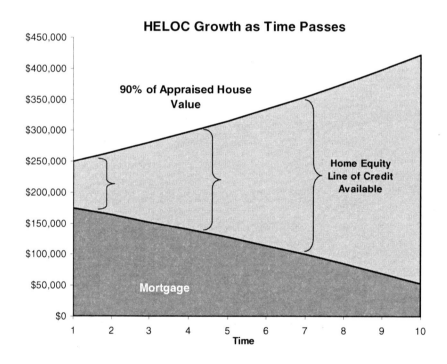

Each year, he got to deduct more and more interest from his business and investment loans. By getting larger and larger interest deductions, he didn't have to pay as much into his third party tax strategy in later years.

The tax refunds stayed just as big, but there was more money for investing because the tax refunds cost him less every year. This translated into more capital each year that he had to invest. This lowered his expenses and increased his portfolio at the same time.

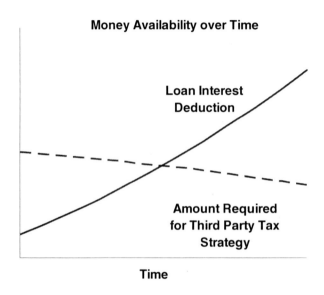

Money Availability over Time

Loan Interest Deduction

Amount Required for Third Party Tax Strategy

Time

As the years passed, his business also generated more revenue. Mike also got really good at deducting business expenses, which provided him more free deductions from his income. As with most good things, the earlier Mike started the strategy, the greater the effects were in the long run.

EFFECTS OF A FULLY PAID HOUSE

Mike knew what the numbers were for his situation with a new mortgage. His friend Lenny wondered what the numbers would be for him, as his house was fully paid off. So Mike crunched the numbers for Lenny, with each step in the system as an option.

To get a good idea of how valuable the parts of the system were, Mike did a side-by-side comparison to see the gain from his system in just one year. He took Lenny's $250,000 fully paid house appreciating at an average rate of 5%, with Lenny's household income of $64,400 at a 25% marginal tax rate.

Option	A	B	C	D
Home Appreciation	$12,500	$12,500	$12,500	$12,500
Investment Return		$50,000	$48,800	$48,440
Tax Reduction			$8,000	$8,000
Home Business				$2,250
Total Gain	**$12,500**	**$62,500**	**$69,300**	**$71,190**

By using every step in his system in this example, Lenny would add over $71,190 to his income in the first year alone, and this figure would grow every year. This wasn't even counting the profits he was making from his home business or extra money he was able to set aside for savings.

Just by matching his saving and investing to what this system was making him, he would quickly accelerate his net worth and reach financial freedom in a only a few years.

The numbers are better for someone like Lenny who already had the house paid off, compared to someone like Mike who started off with a full mortgage. This is because the equity has already been saved up in the house when it is paid off.

For someone like Mike who was just starting off with a mortgage at the beginning of this process, it took more time, but the system still gave a significant boost to his net worth. But irrespective of this, both Mike and Lenny saw massive results in just a few years.

ACTION STEPS

Mike had developed this system that anyone in the middle class could use to get ahead, literally with no money down and very little risk.

Here are newly proclaimed Millionaire Mike's action steps:

- ☐ Have house appraised
- ☐ Determine amount of equity that can be borrowed
- ☐ Find a lender for home equity line of credit
- ☐ Start up home business as a sole proprietor
- ☐ Fund the sole proprietor business with business loan
- ☐ Estimate deductible business expenses
- ☐ Estimate expense-to-core cost ratio
- ☐ Find and fund a third party tax strategy that works
- ☐ Establish ways to protect wealth as it grows
- ☐ Find secure high rate of return investments
- ☐ Use cash to pay down any non-deductible debt
- ☐ Use tax refunds, and loans to invest
- ☐ Enjoy the passive income

Middle Class Mike	Millionaire Mike
Spent money on mortgage and bills	Spent money on mortgage, paying down bad debt, and more mortgage
No $ for business	Business fully funded
No $ for investing	Liberated capital, tax refunds, and loans for investing
No cash in the end	Thousands of dollars in additional cash flow
Will likely have to work to death	Financially free within ten years

PLAN YOUR ESCAPE: A NOTE FROM THE AUTHOR

Mike escaped the middle class traps into financial freedom. Anyone with a house, an income tax bill, consumer expenses, and the desire to have great personal finances automatically qualifies to also take this route.

The concepts in this book are usually radically new and different to most people. Once you understand the concepts fully, it is time for you to put this knowledge to work in your own life, and share these strategies with those around you who also want to become financially free.

I found that it is extremely helpful to have a group of like-minded people with whom you can discuss these strategies. In his book, *Think and Grow Rich*, Napoleon Hill called this a "Mastermind Group." Early in my wealth creation days I joined a like-minded group of individuals with whom I associated. I met with them every Tuesday at lunch to discuss strategies just like this. If you don't already have this group formed in your life, I highly recommend it. You can even use the ideas in this book as a starting point to get the discussion rolling. As your group grows, it may even turn into the team you work with to find and examine opportunities.

I encourage you by all means possible go out to actively seek and discuss more of this type of knowledge from friends, business associates, partners, and mentors, as it is the only path to true freedom.

That's it. That's the story. The rest is up to you. The question is: will you be like Mike?

You can order more copies of this book through your online bookstore, the publisher, or through the website www.yourleverage.com. I also encourage you to share your success story with us, so that we may inspire others to follow your path to freedom.

To your learning and financial freedom!

- Douglas S. Anderson

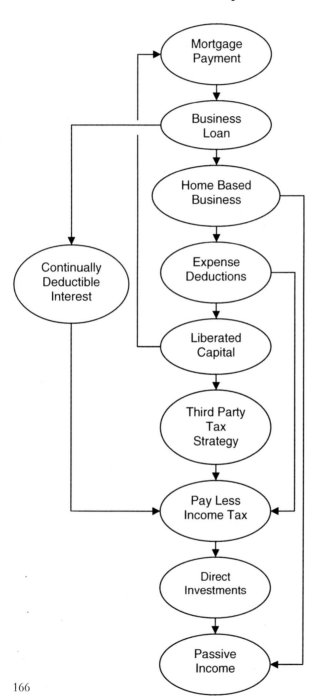

The Entire System

ANNEX A –VARIABLE VERSUS FIXED RATE

Year	Annual Returns Stocks	Compounded Value of $ 100 Variable Rate	Fixed Rate 11%
1928	43.81%	$143.81	$111.72
1929	-8.30%	$131.88	$124.81
1930	-25.12%	$98.75	$139.43
1931	-43.84%	$55.46	$155.76
1932	-8.64%	$50.66	$174.01
1933	49.98%	$75.99	$194.40
1934	-1.19%	$75.09	$217.18
1935	46.74%	$110.18	$242.62
1936	31.94%	$145.38	$271.05
1937	-35.34%	$94.00	$302.81
1938	29.28%	$121.53	$338.28
1939	-1.10%	$120.20	$377.92
1940	-10.67%	$107.37	$422.20
1941	-12.77%	$93.66	$471.66
1942	19.17%	$111.61	$526.92
1943	25.06%	$139.59	$588.66
1944	19.03%	$166.15	$657.63
1945	35.82%	$225.67	$734.68
1946	-8.43%	$206.65	$820.75
1947	5.20%	$217.39	$916.92
1948	5.70%	$229.79	$1,024.34
1949	18.30%	$271.85	$1,144.36
1950	30.81%	$355.60	$1,278.44
1951	23.68%	$439.80	$1,428.22
1952	18.15%	$519.62	$1,595.56
1953	-1.21%	$513.35	$1,782.49
1954	52.56%	$783.18	$1,991.34
1955	32.60%	$1,038.47	$2,224.65
1956	7.44%	$1,115.73	$2,485.29
1957	-10.46%	$999.05	$2,776.48
1958	43.72%	$1,435.84	$3,101.78
1959	12.06%	$1,608.95	$3,465.19
1960	0.34%	$1,614.37	$3,871.18
1961	26.64%	$2,044.40	$4,324.74
1962	-8.81%	$1,864.26	$4,831.44
1963	22.61%	$2,285.80	$5,397.51
1964	16.42%	$2,661.02	$6,029.89
1965	12.40%	$2,990.97	$6,736.37
1966	-9.97%	$2,692.74	$7,525.62

1967	23.80%	$3,333.69	$8,407.35
1968	10.81%	$3,694.23	$9,392.38
1969	-8.24%	$3,389.77	$10,492.81
1970	3.56%	$3,510.49	$11,722.18
1971	14.22%	$4,009.72	$13,095.58
1972	18.76%	$4,761.76	$14,629.90
1973	-14.31%	$4,080.44	$16,343.98
1974	-25.90%	$3,023.54	$18,258.89
1975	37.00%	$4,142.10	$20,398.15
1976	23.83%	$5,129.20	$22,788.05
1977	-6.98%	$4,771.20	$25,457.97
1978	6.51%	$5,081.77	$28,440.69
1979	18.52%	$6,022.89	$31,772.88
1980	31.74%	$7,934.26	$35,495.48
1981	-4.70%	$7,561.16	$39,654.24
1982	20.42%	$9,105.08	$44,300.24
1983	22.34%	$11,138.90	$49,490.58
1984	6.15%	$11,823.51	$55,289.03
1985	31.24%	$15,516.60	$61,766.85
1986	18.49%	$18,386.33	$69,003.63
1987	5.81%	$19,455.08	$77,088.29
1988	16.54%	$22,672.40	$86,120.17
1989	31.48%	$29,808.58	$96,210.26
1990	-3.06%	$28,895.11	$107,482.52
1991	30.23%	$37,631.51	$120,075.48
1992	7.49%	$40,451.51	$134,143.86
1993	9.97%	$44,483.33	$149,860.53
1994	1.33%	$45,073.14	$167,418.62
1995	37.20%	$61,838.19	$187,033.85
1996	23.82%	$76,566.48	$208,947.27
1997	31.86%	$100,958.71	$233,428.12
1998	28.34%	$129,568.35	$260,777.21
1999	20.89%	$156,629.15	$291,330.61
2000	-9.03%	$142,482.69	$325,463.72
2001	-11.85%	$125,598.83	$363,595.97
2002	-21.98%	$97,996.61	$406,195.90
2003	28.41%	$125,838.91	$453,786.96
2004	10.70%	$139,308.83	$506,953.92
2005	4.85%	**$146,062.54**	**$566,350.07**

RRSP - alternative - putting = $100 pm

Becoming a business to rent my property?
     - tax write off

Lower my taxes

Interest rates - history most 2,5,10 40 years
 | └Fixed vs Variable.
what are they going to do?

Ⓧ Calculate Net worth.
        interest only
"Line of Credit" mortgage - will give me 195k, 40k more
L can I get lower then interest rate?
HELOC set up?

3rd party tax strategys.
- paper assets
- hedge funds?

ISBN 142514039-4

9 781425 140397